WILLIAMS-SONOMA

CAKE

RECIPES AND TEXT
FRAN GAGE

GENERAL EDITOR
CHUCK WILLIAMS

PHOTOGRAPHS
NOEL BARNHURST

SIMON & SCHUSTER • **SOURCE**

NEW YORK • LONDON • TORONTO • SYDNEY • SINGAPORE

CONTENTS

SPRING AND SUMMER CAKES

AUTUMN AND WINTER CAKES

DECORATED CAKES

INTRODUCTION

When you take the time to prepare a cake for family and friends, you automatically turn a gathering into a special occasion. Whether you are looking for a cake to conclude a weekday meal or celebrate a birthday in style, I know that you will find a recipe in this book that will both impress your guests and suit your baking experience. Among the 36 kitchen-tested recipes are classic layer cakes and simple cakes like gingerbread, and elegant confections decorated with piped frosting and other embellishments.

Making cakes is certainly an art. Yet, it is also a science. For this reason, before you begin, be sure to read the essential information in the back of the book about the role each ingredient plays, the importance of correctly measuring and mixing ingredients, and the equipment you will need. Additional tips can be found in the recipe side notes, and you will be able to finish your cake with confidence after reading the chapter on decorating cakes. Every facet of this book will surely help you bring artistry and pleasure to your table.

Chuck Williams

THE CLASSICS

These cakes have withstood the test of time. You will find American favorites, such as Pineapple Upside-Down Cake and Carrot Cake, along with European classics like Black Forest Cake and Linzertorte. Choose from cakes layered and frosted with luscious buttercream, or make a light and airy Angel Food Cake embellished with lemon curd.

BIRTHDAY CAKE

ADDING EGGS

One of the secrets to making a good cake is blending the eggs well into the batter. First, start with room-temperature eggs. If they are cold, the batter will separate, resulting in a heavier cake. Second, do not add them directly to the mixer bowl. Instead, crack them into a separate bowl, break them up with a fork, and, with the mixer on medium speed, drizzle them in slowly, stopping frequently to let the batter absorb them. If the batter begins to look curdled, increase the mixer speed to high and beat until the batter looks smooth again.

Preheat the oven to 350°F (180°C). Line the bottoms of two 9-by-2-inch (23-by-5-cm) round cake pans with parchment (baking) paper.

Sift the flour, baking powder, and salt together onto a sheet of waxed paper; set aside. In a small bowl, combine the milk and vanilla; set aside.

Using a stand mixer, beat the butter with the paddle on medium speed until creamy. Add the sugar and beat until the mixture is pale and fluffy. Drizzle in the eggs, beating each addition until incorporated before continuing *(left)*. Reduce the speed to medium-low and add the dry ingredients in 3 additions alternately with the milk mixture in 2 additions, starting and ending with the dry ingredients. Beat just until combined.

Pour the batter into the prepared pans and spread it evenly. Bake until the cakes are puffed and a skewer inserted into the centers comes out clean, 20–25 minutes. Let cool completely on a wire rack. Run a table knife around the edges of the pans and invert the cakes onto plates.

To frost the cake, put one layer, top side down, on a serving plate. Peel off the parchment paper. Using a straight frosting spatula, spread evenly with about a third of the buttercream. Invert the other layer, top side down, on the first layer and peel off the paper. Refrigerate the cake for 30 minutes to firm the frosting; keep the remaining buttercream at room temperature. Spread the butter-cream on the top and sides of the cake (page 111). Refrigerate the cake until 30 minutes before serving to set the frosting.

MAKES 10–12 SERVINGS

2 cups (9 oz/250 g) unbleached all-purpose (plain) flour

2 teaspoons baking powder

¼ teaspoon salt

½ cup (4 fl oz/110 ml) whole milk, at room temperature

2 teaspoons vanilla extract (essence)

1 cup (8 oz/225 g) unsalted butter, at room temperature

1½ cups (10½ oz/300 g) sugar

4 large eggs, at room temperature, lightly beaten

Chocolate Buttercream (page 115)

DEVIL'S FOOD CAKE

1¾ cups (8 oz/225 g)
unbleached all-purpose
(plain) flour

1 teaspoon baking soda
(bicarbonate of soda)

¼ teaspoon salt

½ cup (2 oz/60 g) Dutch-
process cocoa powder
(far right)

½ cup (4 fl oz/110 ml)
hot water

½ cup (4 fl oz/110 ml)
buttermilk, at room
temperature

2 teaspoons vanilla extract
(essence)

¾ cup (6 oz/170 g)
unsalted butter,
at room temperature

1 cup (7 oz/200 g)
granulated sugar

½ cup (3 oz/85 g) firmly
packed light brown sugar

3 large eggs, at room
temperature, lightly beaten

4 cups (32 fl oz/900 ml)
Coffee Meringue
Buttercream (page 114)

Preheat the oven to 350°F (180°C). Line the bottoms of two 9-by-2-inch (23-by-5-cm) round cake pans with parchment (baking) paper.

Sift the flour, baking soda, and salt together onto a sheet of waxed paper; set aside. In a bowl, whisk the cocoa powder into the hot water. Let cool to lukewarm, then whisk in the buttermilk and vanilla. Set aside.

Using a stand mixer, beat the butter with the paddle on medium speed until creamy. Add the granulated and brown sugars and beat until the mixture is pale and fluffy. Slowly drizzle in the eggs, beating each addition until incorporated before continuing (page 10). Reduce the speed to medium-low and add the dry ingredients in 3 additions alternately with the buttermilk mixture in 2 additions, starting and ending with the dry ingredients. Beat just until combined.

Pour the batter into the prepared pans and smooth the top. Bake until the cakes are puffed and slightly springy to the touch, and a skewer inserted into the centers comes out clean, 25–30 minutes. Let cool completely on a wire rack. Run a table knife around the edges of the pans and invert the cakes onto plates.

To frost the cake, put one layer, top side down, on a serving plate. Peel off the parchment paper. Using a straight frosting spatula, spread evenly with about a third of the buttercream. Invert the other layer, top side down, on the first layer and peel off the paper. Refrigerate the cake for 30 minutes to firm the frosting; keep the remaining buttercream at room temperature. Spread the butter-cream on the top and sides of the cake (page 111). Make wavy lines with a decorating comb across the top of the cake, then make lines around its sides (page 97). Refrigerate the cake until 30 minutes before serving to set the frosting.

MAKES 10–12 SERVINGS

COCOA POWDER

Chocolate is made by crushing roasted cocoa beans into bits, or nibs, to produce what is known as chocolate liquor. To make unsweetened cocoa powder, much of the cocoa butter (the fat of chocolate) is removed from the liquor and what remains is ground. Dutch-process cocoa, or alkalized cocoa, has a mild flavor and a rich, dark color due to the addition of potassium carbonate; nonalkalized cocoa has a bolder taste and lighter color. Dutch-process cocoa reacts with the baking soda in devil's food cake batter to give the cake its distinctive reddish brown color.

ANGEL FOOD CAKE

Preheat the oven to 350°F (180°C). Have ready an ungreased angel food cake pan 10 inches (25 cm) in diameter and 4 inches (10 cm) deep.

Sift the flour, confectioners' sugar, and salt together twice onto a sheet of waxed paper; set aside.

Using a stand mixer, beat the egg whites with the whisk on medium speed until they start to foam. Add a third of the superfine sugar and beat until the whites are opaque, then add another third of the sugar and the cream of tartar and continue beating. When the whites start to increase in volume and become firm, add the remaining sugar and the vanilla and increase the speed to high. Beat just until the whites form very soft peaks *(left)*. Do not overbeat. Remove the bowl from the mixer. Sift a third of the dry ingredients over the egg whites and carefully fold in with a large rubber spatula. Sift and fold in the remaining dry ingredients in 2 more additions.

Pour the batter into the pan and smooth the top. Bake until the top of the cake is lightly browned and feels springy when touched, and a skewer inserted into the center of the cake comes out clean, 40–45 minutes. Immediately invert the cake onto a countertop if the pan has feet or, if it does not, over the neck of a wine bottle. Let cool completely. Tap the pan on a counter to release the cake, then invert it onto a serving plate. If necessary, run a thin-bladed knife around the outer sides of the pan and around the inside of the tube.

To serve, cut the cake with a very thin serrated knife. Accompany each slice with lemon curd or raspberry purée.

MAKES 10–12 SERVINGS

WHIPPING EGG WHITES

Whipped egg whites act as the leavening for angel food and other sponge cakes. For successful whipping, the bowl and beaters must be perfectly clean, because even a trace of fat prevents good loft. It is also important to start with room-temperature whites. Sugar and/or cream of tartar is often added during whipping to help stabilize the whites.

To test if the whites are whipped to the desired finish, lift the beaters: soft peaks should droop over gently and look wet; medium-firm peaks should stand upright but still appear moist and satiny.

1 cup (4 oz/110 g) cake (soft-wheat) flour

1 cup (3½ oz/100 g) confectioners' (icing) sugar

¼ teaspoon salt

12 large egg whites, at room temperature

¾ cup (5 oz/140 g) superfine (caster) sugar

1½ teaspoons cream of tartar

1½ teaspoons vanilla extract (essence)

Lemon Curd (page 115) or Raspberry Purée (page 115) for serving

CARROT CAKE

¾ cup (3 oz/85 g) walnuts

¾ lb (335 g) carrots

1¼ cups (6 oz/170 g) unbleached all-purpose (plain) flour

2 teaspoons baking powder

½ teaspoon *each* baking soda (bicarbonate of soda) and salt

1 teaspoon ground cinnamon

½ teaspoon freshly grated nutmeg *(far right)*

2 large eggs

1⅓ cups (8 oz/225 g) firmly packed light brown sugar

½ cup (4 fl oz/110 ml) whole milk

½ cup (4 oz/110 g) unsalted butter, melted and cooled to room temperature

½ cup (2½ oz/70 g) dried currants

FOR THE FROSTING:

4 oz (110 g) cream cheese

2 tablespoons unsalted butter

¾ cup (3 oz/85 g) confectioners' (icing) sugar

¾ teaspoon vanilla extract (essence)

Lightly toast the walnuts (page 47) and then coarsely chop; set aside. Peel the carrots and cut into ½-inch (12-mm) slices.

Bring a large saucepan three-fourths full of water to a boil. Add the carrots and cook until tender, 10–15 minutes. Drain and let cool. In a food processor, purée the cooked carrots. You should have about 1 cup (8 fl oz/225 ml) purée.

Preheat the oven to 350°F (180°C). Line the bottom of an 8-inch (20-cm) square baking pan with parchment (baking) paper.

Sift the flour, baking powder, baking soda, salt, cinnamon, and nutmeg together onto a sheet of waxed paper; set aside.

In a large bowl, whisk together the eggs and brown sugar until well combined. Whisk in the milk and melted butter. Whisk in the dry ingredients and then the carrot purée. Using a large rubber spatula, stir in the walnuts and currants.

Pour the batter into the prepared pan and smooth the top. Bake until lightly browned and a skewer inserted into the center comes out clean, 45–50 minutes. Let cool completely on a wire rack. Run a table knife around the edge of the pan and invert the cake onto a serving plate. Peel off the parchment paper.

To make the frosting, using a stand mixer, beat the cream cheese, butter, confectioners' sugar, and vanilla with the paddle on medium speed until combined. Using a straight frosting spatula, spread the frosting on the top and sides of the cake (page 111). Refrigerate the cake if not serving it immediately. Remove it from the refrigerator 30 minutes before serving.

MAKES 9 SERVINGS

NUTMEG

Native to the East Indies, highly aromatic nutmeg is one of the oldest cultivated spices. It is the hard stone of the fruit of the nutmeg tree and is covered with a lacy, red webbing that is harvested as a separate spice, mace. Once nutmeg is grated, its volatile oils quickly begin to evaporate and its flavor diminishes, so buy whole nutmegs, rather than preground, and grate as needed. Use a nutmeg grater, a tool with fine, sharp rasps and a small compartment for storing one or two nutmegs, or the finest rasps on a shredder-grater.

COCONUT LAYER CAKE

Preheat the oven to 350°F (180°C). Line the bottoms of two 9-by-2-inch (23-by-5-cm) round cake pans with parchment (baking) paper.

Sift the flour, baking powder, and salt together onto a sheet of waxed paper; set aside. In a small bowl, combine the coconut milk and vanilla. Set aside.

Using a stand mixer, beat the butter with the paddle on medium speed until creamy. Add the sugar and beat until the mixture is pale and fluffy. Slowly drizzle in the eggs, beating each addition until incorporated before continuing (page 10). Reduce the speed to medium-low and add the dry ingredients in 3 additions alternately with the coconut milk mixture in 2 additions, starting and ending with the dry ingredients. Beat just until combined.

Pour the batter into the prepared pans and smooth the top. Bake until the cake is puffed and a skewer inserted into the centers comes out clean, 20–25 minutes. Let cool completely on a wire rack. Run a table knife around the edges of the pans and invert the cakes onto plates.

To frost the cake, put one layer, top side down, on a serving plate. Peel off the parchment paper. In a small bowl, mix a fourth of the coconut with about a third of the buttercream and, using a straight frosting spatula, spread it evenly on top. Invert the other layer, top side down, onto the first layer and peel off the paper. Refrigerate the cake for 30 minutes to firm the frosting; keep the remaining buttercream at room temperature. Spread the buttercream on the top and sides of the cake (page 111). Press the remaining coconut onto the sides of the cake. Refrigerate the cake until 30 minutes before serving to set the frosting.

MAKES 10–12 SERVINGS

COCONUT

Coconut milk, which is made by soaking grated coconut in water, is sold in cans or frozen in well-stocked grocery stores. It is available in full-fat and reduced-fat forms (use the former for this recipe). Do not confuse it with sweetened coconut cream, sometimes labeled "cream of coconut." Use unsweetened desiccated, or dried, coconut for the buttercream and for decorating the sides of the cake. To toast dried coconut, spread on a baking pan lined with parchment (baking) paper and toast in a 350°F (180°C) oven for about 3 minutes.

2 cups (9 oz/250 g) unbleached all-purpose (plain) flour

2 teaspoons baking powder

¼ teaspoon salt

½ cup (4 fl oz/110 ml) coconut milk, at room temperature

2 teaspoons vanilla extract (essence)

1 cup (8 oz/225 g) unsalted butter, at room temperature

1½ cups (10½ oz/300 g) sugar

4 large eggs, at room temperature, lightly beaten

1 cup (2½ oz/70 g) unsweetened shredded coconut

Vanilla Buttercream (page 115)

PINEAPPLE UPSIDE-DOWN CAKE

½ cup (4 oz/110 g) plus
2 tablespoons unsalted
butter, at room temperature

1¼ cups (9 oz/250 g) sugar

5 slices peeled fresh
pineapple, each ½ inch
(12 mm) thick, cored and
cut into quarters *(far right)*

1½ cups (7 oz/200 g)
unbleached all-purpose
(plain) flour

1½ teaspoons baking
powder

¼ teaspoon salt

2 large eggs, at room
temperature, lightly beaten

¾ cup (6 fl oz/170 ml)
buttermilk, at room
temperature

1 tablespoon dark rum

In a 9-by-3-inch (23-by-7.5-cm) round, heavy aluminum cake pan over medium heat, melt the 2 tablespoons butter. Add ½ cup (3½ oz/100 g) of the sugar and heat, stirring occasionally, until the sugar melts and turns light brown, 5–7 minutes. Add the pineapple and arrange the slices decoratively. Cook, without stirring, until the pineapple releases its juice and the sugar is a medium caramel color, about 5 minutes.

Preheat the oven to 350°F (180°C). Sift the flour, baking powder, and salt together onto a sheet of waxed paper; set aside.

Using a stand mixer, beat the ½ cup butter with the paddle on medium speed until creamy. Add the remaining ¾ cup (5½ oz/150 g) sugar and beat until the mixture is pale and fluffy. Slowly drizzle in the eggs, beating each addition until incorporated before continuing (page 10). Reduce the speed to medium-low and add the dry ingredients in 3 additions alternately with the buttermilk in 2 additions, starting and ending with the dry ingredients. Beat just until combined. Beat in the rum.

Pour the batter on top of the pineapple and spread it evenly to the edge of the pan. Bake until the top is browned, 30–40 minutes. Let cool on a wire rack for 10 minutes.

Run a table knife around the edge of the pan and shake it to make sure the cake is not sticking to the bottom. (If it is, set the pan over low heat and heat for 1–2 minutes, gently shaking the pan until the cake is free.) Place a serving platter upside down on the pan. Wearing oven mitts, invert the platter and pan together. Lift off the pan. Dislodge any pineapple pieces that stick to the pan and arrange on top of the cake. Serve at room temperature.

MAKES 8–10 SERVINGS

PREPARING PINEAPPLE
A ripe pineapple is fragrant and golden and gives slightly when pressed. To peel the fruit, cut off the green top and a thin slice from the bottom. Stand the fruit upright and, using a large, sharp knife, cut the peel away in vertical strips. Lay the pineapple on its side and align the blade with the diagonal rows of brown "eyes." Working in a spiral, cut in at an angle on each side of the eyes to remove them. To slice the fruit, cut crosswise. Remove the core from each slice with a small cookie cutter, an apple corer, or a paring knife.

BLACK FOREST CAKE

Preheat the oven to 350°F (180°C). Line the bottom of a 9-by-3-inch (23-by-7.5-cm) round cake pan with parchment (baking) paper.

Sift the flour and cocoa powder together onto a sheet of waxed paper; set aside. Using a stand mixer, beat the eggs, vanilla, and granulated sugar with the whisk on high speed until tripled in volume, about 5 minutes. Remove the bowl from the mixer. Sift the dry ingredients over the egg mixture in 2 additions and carefully fold in with a large rubber spatula. Fold a large dollop into the melted butter, then fold back into the egg mixture. Pour into the prepared pan and smooth the top. Bake until the cake is puffed, 30–35 minutes. Let cool completely on a wire rack.

Meanwhile, make the filling and frosting: Whip the cream and confectioners' sugar to medium-stiff peaks (page 80). In a small bowl, combine the kirsch and sugar syrup.

Run a table knife around the edge of the pan and unmold the cake onto a work surface. Turn right side up, leaving the parchment paper in place. Cut the cake into 3 equal layers (page 48). Put the top layer, cut side up, on a serving plate. Brush with some of the syrup, then spread with about a fourth of the whipped cream. Strew the cherries over the cream (reserve one for garnish), leaving a ½-inch (12-mm) border of cream around the edge. Position the middle layer on the cream. Brush with some of the syrup and spread with another fourth of the cream. Position the third layer, cut side down, on the cream and peel off the paper. Brush with the remaining syrup. Spread the remaining whipped cream on the top and sides of the cake (page 111).

Press the chocolate curls onto the top of the cake. Put the reserved cherry in the middle. Refrigerate until ready to serve.

MAKES 8–10 SERVINGS

POACHED CHERRIES

A filling of cherries and kirsch-flavored whipped cream is standard in this classic German cake. To poach the cherries, in a small saucepan over medium heat, bring 1¾ cups (14 fl oz/ 390 ml) water and ⅓ cup (2½ oz/70 g) granulated sugar to a boil, stirring occasionally. Add 1 cup (6 oz/170 g) fresh pitted Bing or other dark sweet cherries, reduce the heat to low, and cook until soft, about 10 minutes. Let the cherries cool, then drain; discard the syrup. Frozen or jarred cherries may also be used. Cook the frozen cherries as directed above. Jarred cherries have already been poached.

½ cup (2 oz/60 g) cake (soft-wheat) flour

½ cup (2 oz/60 g) Dutch-process cocoa powder (page 13)

6 large eggs, at room temperature

1 teaspoon vanilla extract (essence)

¾ cup (5½ oz/155 g) granulated sugar

½ cup (4 oz/110 g) unsalted butter, melted and cooled to room temperature

FOR THE FILLING AND FROSTING:

2½ cups (20 fl oz/560 ml) heavy (double) cream

2 tablespoons confectioners' (icing) sugar

1 teaspoon kirsch

Sugar Syrup (page 55)

Poached cherries *(far left)*

Semisweet (plain) chocolate curls (page 102)

LINZERTORTE

1½ cups (7 oz/200 g) unbleached all-purpose (plain) flour

¼ teaspoon ground cinnamon

⅛ teaspoon ground cloves

¼ teaspoon salt

1 lemon

1 cup (5½ oz/155 g) unblanched whole almonds

1 cup (3½ oz/100 g) confectioners' (icing) sugar, plus extra for dusting

¾ cup (6 oz/170 g) unsalted butter, at room temperature

3 large egg yolks

1½ cups (18 oz/500 g) raspberry jam

1 tablespoon whole milk

Sift the flour, cinnamon, cloves, and salt into a bowl. Using the finest holes of a handheld grater, grate the zest from the lemon into the bowl. Set aside. In a food processor, process the almonds with the 1 cup confectioners' sugar until finely ground. Set aside.

Using a stand mixer, beat the butter with the paddle on medium speed until creamy. Beat in the almond mixture, then 2 of the egg yolks. Reduce the speed to low, add the dry ingredients, and beat just until combined. Flatten about a third of the dough into a disk, wrap in plastic, and refrigerate. Butter a 9-by-1-inch (23-by-2.5-cm) round fluted tart pan with a removable bottom. Using your fingers, press the remaining dough into the bottom and sides of the pan, extending it ½ inch (12 mm) above the top. If the dough is overly soft and sticky, refrigerate it until firm enough to continue. Spread the dough with the jam.

On a lightly floured surface, roll the chilled dough into a rectangle about 9 inches (23 cm) long and ¼ inch (6 mm) thick. Using a fluted pastry cutter, cut into 6 strips, each 1 inch (2.5 cm) wide; 2 of them should be 9 inches (23 cm) long and the others slightly shorter. Lay the strips on the torte *(right)*, trimming the edges. Fold the dough extending above the pan back over the filling and strips. Crimp to seal the edges. Place the torte in the freezer for 20 minutes. Preheat the oven to 350°F (180°C).

In a small bowl, whisk together the remaining egg yolk and the milk. Brush the dough with the yolk mixture. Bake until the crust is browned and the jam is bubbling, 45–55 minutes. Let cool on a wire rack until the torte is barely warm. Remove the pan sides. Run a thin-bladed knife between the torte and the pan bottom. Transfer the torte to a serving plate and let cool completely. Just before serving, dust the torte with confectioners' sugar, if desired.

MAKES 8–10 SERVINGS

LATTICE CRUST
An eighteenth-century specialty of the Austrian town of Linz, the almond-rich Linzertorte is identifiable by its decorative latticework top. To make the lattice, roll out the dough and cut into strips as directed in the recipe. Lay a long strip across the center of the torte. Set a shorter strip on each side of the center strip, equidistant from the center strip and the edge of the torte. Place the second long strip diagonally across the first strips, again in the center of the torte. Place the remaining shorter strips on either side, then proceed as directed.

SIMPLE CAKES

Everyone needs a few cake recipes in their repertoire that can be made quickly for an impromptu dinner party or as a treat for the family. This chapter features recipes for all seasons in a variety of flavors, including chocolate cupcakes, an almond cake baked in a Bundt pan, a rich chocolate torte, and an aromatic spice cake studded with golden raisins.

CINNAMON-APPLESAUCE CAKE

BRIOCHE MOLD

Baking this spiced applesauce cake in a traditional brioche mold, which is round and fluted and wider at the top than at the bottom, gives the cake the same distinctive shape as the popular, yeast-risen French breakfast bread that shares the mold's name. Available in a wide range of sizes, the molds were introduced in the nineteenth century (although the brioche dough enriched with egg and butter has existed much longer).

Preheat the oven to 325°F (165°C). Generously butter a 5-cup (40–fl oz/1.1-l) brioche mold. Sift the flour, salt, cinnamon, nutmeg, and baking powder together onto a sheet of waxed paper; set aside.

Using a stand mixer, beat the butter with the paddle on medium speed until creamy. Add the brown sugar and beat until the mixture is pale and fluffy. Slowly drizzle in the eggs, beating each addition until incorporated before continuing (page 10). Reduce the mixer speed to medium-low and add the dry ingredients in 3 additions alternately with the applesauce in 2 additions, starting and ending with the dry ingredients. Beat just until combined. With a large rubber spatula, fold in the walnuts.

Pour the batter into the prepared mold and smooth the top. Bake for 40 minutes, then cover with aluminum foil. Continue to bake until the cake is puffed and a skewer inserted into the center comes out clean, 20–25 minutes longer. Let the cake cool on a wire rack until the mold is cool to the touch. Tap the mold on a counter to release the cake, then invert it onto a serving plate.

Meanwhile, to make the topping, in a bowl, stir together the sour cream, confectioners' sugar, and cinnamon.

Serve each slice with a spoonful of sour cream topping.

MAKES 8 SERVINGS

1½ cups (7 oz/200 g) unbleached all-purpose (plain) flour

¼ teaspoon salt

1½ teaspoons ground cinnamon

½ teaspoon freshly grated nutmeg (page 17)

1½ teaspoons baking powder

½ cup (4 oz/110 g) unsalted butter, at room temperature

1¼ cups (7½ oz/210 g) firmly packed light brown sugar

2 large eggs, at room temperature, lightly beaten

¾ cup (7 oz/200 g) smooth unsweetened applesauce, at room temperature

½ cup (2 oz/60 g) walnuts, lightly toasted (page 47) and coarsely chopped

FOR THE SOUR CREAM TOPPING:

1 cup (8 oz/225 g) sour cream

1 tablespoon confectioners' (icing) sugar

¼ teaspoon ground cinnamon

ESPRESSO POUND CAKE

1½ cups (7 oz/200 g) unbleached all-purpose (plain) flour

1 teaspoon baking powder

¼ teaspoon salt

1 tablespoon finely ground dark-roast coffee beans *(far right)*

1 lemon

⅔ cup (5 oz/140 g) unsalted butter, at room temperature

1 cup (7 oz/200 g) sugar

2 large eggs, at room temperature, lightly beaten

⅓ cup (3 fl oz/80 ml) buttermilk, at room temperature

Preheat the oven to 350°F (180°C). Generously butter an 8½-by-4½-inch (21.5-by-11.5-cm) loaf pan.

Sift the flour, baking powder, and salt together into a bowl. Stir in the ground coffee. Using the finest rasps of a handheld grater, grate the zest from the lemon into the bowl. Set aside.

Using a stand mixer, beat the butter with the paddle on medium speed until creamy. Add the sugar and beat until the mixture is pale and fluffy. Slowly drizzle in the eggs, beating each addition until incorporated before continuing (page 10). Reduce the speed to medium-low and add the dry ingredients in 3 additions alternately with the buttermilk in 2 additions, starting and ending with the dry ingredients. Beat just until combined.

Pour the batter into the prepared pan and smooth the top. Bake until the cake is browned and puffed, and a skewer inserted into the center comes out clean, 50–60 minutes. Let cool completely on a wire rack. Run a table knife around the edge of the pan and turn the cake out onto a serving plate. Place the cake right side up.

Serving Tip: Try this pound cake for breakfast or with a cup of tea in the afternoon.

MAKES 8–10 SERVINGS

COFFEE

Many cake batters flavored with coffee call for brewed coffee, but this pound cake uses ground roasted beans, for a more robust coffee taste. Choose dark-roasted beans, such as French, Italian, or espresso roast, and buy them from a shop that roasts frequently and has a steady turnover of inventory. For the best flavor, grind the beans to as fine a powder as possible. If you do not have a coffee grinder, buy coffee beans within a day of baking the cake and ask the shop to grind them for you.

CHOCOLATE-ORANGE CUPCAKES

MELTING CHOCOLATE

To melt chocolate, chop it into small pieces and put it in a stainless-steel bowl. Set the bowl in a saucepan over, but not touching, barely simmering water. Heat until the chocolate melts, stirring occasionally. Do not allow any water or steam to come in contact with the chocolate, or it will become stiff and grainy. Or, chop the chocolate in large pieces, place in a microwave-safe dish, and microwave on low for 1 minute. Continue to microwave if necessary, checking every 20 seconds, until the chocolate looks softened, then stir until smooth and liquid.

Preheat the oven to 350°F (180°C). Line 12 standard muffin cups with paper liners.

In a small bowl, stir the cocoa powder into the hot water until it dissolves; set aside. Sift the flour, baking powder, baking soda, and salt together into a bowl. Using the finest rasps of a handheld grater, grate the zest from the orange into the bowl. Set aside.

In a large bowl, whisk together the eggs and granulated sugar until well combined. Whisk in the buttermilk and vanilla, then the dissolved cocoa. Whisk in the melted butter, then the dry ingredients.

Using a tablespoon, divide the batter among the muffin cups, filling each about half full. Bake until the cupcakes are puffed and a skewer inserted into the center of one comes out clean, 15–20 minutes. Let cool completely on a wire rack. Remove the cupcakes from the pan.

To make the frosting, melt the chocolate and let cool to room temperature *(left)*. Meanwhile, using a stand mixer, beat the butter and confectioners' sugar with the paddle on medium speed until creamy and smooth, about 3 minutes. Beat in the melted chocolate until combined. Fill a pastry bag fitted with a ½-inch (12-mm) star tip with the frosting and pipe a spiral on top of each cupcake (page 98). Refrigerate the cupcakes until 30 minutes before serving to set the frosting.

MAKES 12 CUPCAKES

3 tablespoons Dutch-process cocoa powder (page 13)

¼ cup (2 fl oz/60 ml) hot water

1¼ cups (6 oz/170 g) unbleached all-purpose (plain) flour

½ teaspoon *each* baking powder and baking soda (bicarbonate of soda)

¼ teaspoon salt

1 orange

2 large eggs, at room temperature

¾ cup (5½ oz/155 g) granulated sugar

½ cup (4 fl oz/110 ml) buttermilk, at room temperature

½ teaspoon vanilla extract (essence)

¼ cup (2 oz/60 g) unsalted butter, melted and cooled to room temperature

FOR THE FROSTING:

6 oz (170 g) bittersweet chocolate

1 cup (8 oz/225 g) unsalted butter, at room temperature

2 cups (7 oz/200 g) confectioners' (icing) sugar

YOGURT CAKE WITH PEACH PURÉE

FOR THE PEACH PURÉE:

6 ripe peaches, about 1½ lb (670 g) total weight, peeled *(far right)*

About ¼ cup (2 oz/60 g) sugar

FOR THE YOGURT CAKE:

2 cups (9 oz/250 g) unbleached all-purpose (plain) flour

1½ teaspoons baking powder

¼ teaspoon salt

2 large eggs, at room temperature

1 cup (7 oz/200 g) sugar

1 cup (8 oz/225 g) whole-milk plain yogurt, at room temperature

½ teaspoon almond extract (essence)

¼ cup (2 oz/60 g) unsalted butter, melted and cooled to room temperature

To make the peach purée, cut the peeled peaches from the pits. In a food processor or blender, purée the peaches until smooth. Add the sugar to taste. Set aside (see Note).

To make the yogurt cake, preheat the oven to 350°F (180°C). Line the bottom of a 9-by-3-inch (23-by-7.5-cm) round cake pan with parchment (baking) paper.

Sift the flour, baking powder, and salt together onto a sheet of waxed paper; set aside.

In a large bowl, whisk together the eggs and sugar until well combined. Whisk in the yogurt and almond extract, then the melted butter. Whisk in the dry ingredients.

Pour the batter into the prepared pan and smooth the top. Bake until the cake is puffed and browned, and a skewer inserted into the center comes out clean, 30–40 minutes. Let cool completely on a wire rack. Run a table knife around the edge of the pan and invert the cake onto a serving plate. Peel off the parchment paper and place the cake right side up.

Drizzle each serving with peach purée.

Note: If not serving the cake immediately, refrigerate the peach purée. Bring to room temperature before using.

Variation Tip: Nectarines, with the peels intact, may be used in place of the peaches.

MAKES 8–10 SERVINGS

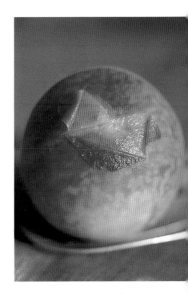

PEELING PEACHES

Before puréeing peaches, remove their skins by blanching. Bring a large saucepan three-fourths full of water to a boil; have ready a bowl of ice water. Cut a shallow X in the blossom end of each peach. Immerse the peaches, two at a time, into the boiling water until their skins start to pull away from the Xs, 5–10 seconds. Using tongs or a slotted spoon, lift them out and immediately plunge them into the ice water, then slip off the skins. Use a paring knife if needed.

ALMOST FLOURLESS CHOCOLATE TORTE

7 oz (200 g) 70-percent
bittersweet chocolate
(far left), finely chopped

14 tablespoons (7 oz/200 g)
unsalted butter, cut into
chunks

1 cup (7 oz/200 g)
superfine (caster) sugar

5 large eggs, separated,
at room temperature

2 tablespoons unbleached
all-purpose (plain) flour

⅛ teaspoon salt

Confectioners' (icing) sugar
for dusting

Dutch-process cocoa
powder (page 13)
for dusting

Raspberry Purée (page
115) for serving

Preheat the oven to 350°F (180°C). Line the bottom of a 9-by-3-inch (23-by-7.5-cm) round cake pan with parchment (baking) paper.

Combine the chocolate and butter in a stainless-steel bowl and melt over, but not touching, barely simmering water (page 32). Remove from the heat and whisk to combine. Whisk in ⅔ cup (4½ oz/125 g) of the superfine sugar and the egg yolks, then whisk in the flour and salt. Set aside.

Using a stand mixer, beat the egg whites with the whisk on medium speed until they start to foam. Add a third of the remaining ⅓ cup (2½ oz/75 g) superfine sugar and beat until the whites are opaque, then add another third of the sugar. When the whites start to increase in volume and become firm, add the remaining sugar and increase the speed to high. Beat until the whites form soft peaks but still look wet (page 14). Using a large rubber spatula, carefully fold a third of the whites into the chocolate mixture, then fold in the remaining whites.

Pour the batter into the prepared pan and smooth the top. Bake until a skewer inserted into the center comes out clean or with only a few crumbs clinging to it, 35–40 minutes. Let the torte cool completely on a wire rack. Run a table knife around the edge of the pan and invert the torte onto a serving plate. Peel off the parchment paper.

Decorate the torte with confectioners' sugar and cocoa powder, creating a two-tone design (page 94). To serve, decorate individual plates with the raspberry purée and place a slice of chocolate torte on each plate.

MAKES 8 SERVINGS

BITTERSWEET CHOCOLATE

Dark chocolates, including bittersweet and semisweet, are a combination of chocolate liquor (essentially the processed kernels of cocoa beans), extra cocoa butter (in addition to what is naturally present in the liquor), and sugar, which determines their sweetness. Good-quality brands, such as Valrhona, Callebaut, and Scharffen Berger, are typically labeled with the percentage of chocolate liquor and cocoa butter; for example, a product that bears a label indicating 70-percent chocolate contains 70 percent liquor and cocoa butter and 30 percent sugar.

ALMOND CAKE

2 cups (9 oz/250 g) unbleached all-purpose (plain) flour

1½ teaspoons baking powder

¼ teaspoon salt

7 oz (200 g) almond paste *(far right)*

¾ cup (6 oz/170 g) unsalted butter, at room temperature

1 cup (7 oz/200 g) sugar

1 teaspoon almond extract (essence)

3 large eggs, at room temperature, lightly beaten

½ cup (4 fl oz/110 ml) buttermilk, at room temperature

Preheat the oven to 350°F (180°C). Generously butter a 9-cup (72–fl oz/2-l) Bundt pan.

Sift the flour, baking powder, and salt together onto a sheet of waxed paper; set aside.

Using a stand mixer, beat the almond paste and butter with the paddle on medium speed until combined. Add the sugar and beat until the mixture is pale and fluffy. Beat in the almond extract. Slowly drizzle in the eggs, beating each addition until incorporated before continuing (page 10). Reduce the speed to medium-low and add the dry ingredients in 3 additions alternately with the buttermilk in 2 additions, starting and ending with the dry ingredients. Beat just until combined.

Pour the batter into the prepared pan and smooth the top. Bake until the cake is browned and puffed, and a skewer inserted into the center comes out clean, 40–50 minutes. Let cool completely on a wire rack. Tap the pan on a counter to release the cake, then invert it onto a serving plate.

Serving Tip: Serve this cake with slices of ripe stone fruit, such as peaches and plums, or with slices of pears.

MAKES 8–10 SERVINGS

ALMOND PASTE

Almond paste is a mixture of ground sweet almonds, water, sugar, and glucose cooked together until a paste forms. The best pastes, packaged in 7-ounce (200-g) logs sold in grocery stores, are at least 50 percent almonds. They add to the moistness of cakes and other desserts and deliver a distinct almond taste that is not possible with ground nuts alone. Marzipan is similar to almond paste but contains a higher percentage of sugar, resulting in a less bold almond taste. It is also more malleable, which makes it popular for rolling into sheets and then draping over cakes.

SPICE CAKE WITH GOLDEN RAISINS

Preheat the oven to 350°F (180°C). Line the bottom of a 9-by-3-inch (23-by-7.5-cm) round cake pan with parchment (baking) paper.

Sift the flour, baking powder, coriander, allspice, salt, cinnamon, and cayenne together onto a sheet of waxed paper; set aside. In a small bowl, combine the milk and vanilla; set aside.

Using a stand mixer, beat the ¾ cup butter with the paddle on medium speed until creamy. Add the brown sugar and the ½ cup granulated sugar and beat until the mixture is pale and fluffy. Slowly drizzle in the eggs, beating each addition until incorporated before continuing (page 10). Reduce the speed to medium-low and add the dry ingredients in 3 additions alternately with the milk mixture in 2 additions, starting and ending with the dry ingredients. Beat just until combined. Fold in the raisins.

Pour the batter into the prepared pan and smooth the top. Bake until the cake is browned and puffed, and a skewer inserted into the center comes out clean, 35–40 minutes. Let cool completely on a wire rack placed over a sheet of waxed paper. Run a table knife around the edge of the pan and invert the cake onto the rack. Peel off the parchment paper and turn the cake right side up.

In a small saucepan, combine the 2 tablespoons granulated sugar, the honey, and the 1 tablespoon butter. Bring to a boil over medium heat, stirring constantly, and cook for about 3 minutes to make a glaze. Pour over the cake. With a small offset frosting spatula, smooth the glaze on the top and sides. Transfer the cake to a serving plate.

Variation Tip: Other dried fruits, such as currants, cranberries, or cherries, may be used in place of the raisins.

MAKES 8–10 SERVINGS

SPICES

Coriander and cayenne are seasonings not commonly found in recipes for sweets, but in this cake they add an intriguing earthiness, and in the case of the cayenne, a subtle spark that is nicely counterbalanced by the honey glaze. Because ground spices lose their potency over time, buy them in small quantities. Better yet, invest in an inexpensive coffee grinder and use it exclusively to grind whole spices, including all of those for this cake, just before use. A mortar and pestle and a steady effort will also reduce whole spices to a powder.

2 cups (9 oz/250 g) unbleached all-purpose (plain) flour

2 teaspoons baking powder

¾ teaspoon *each* ground coriander and ground allspice

½ teaspoon *each* salt and ground cinnamon

¼ teaspoon ground cayenne pepper

¾ cup (6 fl oz/170 ml) whole milk, at room temperature

1 teaspoon vanilla extract (essence)

¾ cup (6 oz/170 g) plus 1 tablespoon unsalted butter, at room temperature

1 cup (6 oz/170 g) firmly packed dark brown sugar

½ cup (3½ oz/100 g) plus 2 tablespoons granulated sugar

2 large eggs, at room temperature, lightly beaten

½ cup (2 oz/60 g) golden raisins (sultanas)

¼ cup (2 oz/60 g) honey

ELEGANT CAKES

When a dazzling dessert is in order, these recipes will help you celebrate in grand style. The chocolate-almond cake and hazelnut cake will satisfy the most ardent chocolate lovers, while the individual vacherins, or meringues, and the dacquoises will make an elegant finale to a fine meal. All of these desserts can be made ahead, so you will be free to join in the festivities.

CHOCOLATE-ALMOND CAKE
WITH CARAMEL SAUCE

Preheat the oven to 325°F (165°C). Butter and flour a 9½-inch (24-cm) savarin mold (page 112).

Combine the chocolate and butter in a stainless-steel bowl and melt over, but not touching, simmering water (page 32). Remove from the heat and whisk to combine. Whisk in ¾ cup (5 oz/140 g) of the superfine sugar, the egg yolks, and the almond extract. In a food processor, process the flour, salt, and almonds until finely ground; do not overprocess. Whisk the flour mixture into the chocolate mixture.

Using a stand mixer, beat the egg whites with the whisk on medium speed until they start to foam. Add a third of the remaining ¼ cup (2 oz/60 g) superfine sugar and beat until the whites are opaque, then add another third of the sugar. When the whites start to increase in volume and become firm, add the remaining sugar and increase the speed to high. Beat until the whites form soft peaks but still look wet (page 14). Using a large rubber spatula, carefully fold a third of the whites into the chocolate mixture, then fold in the remaining whites *(left)*.

Pour the batter into the prepared mold and smooth the top. Bake until the cake is puffed and a skewer inserted into the center comes out clean or with only a few crumbs clinging to it, 40–45 minutes. Let cool on a wire rack to room temperature. Run a table knife around the edges of the mold and tap the bottom on a countertop to release the cake. Invert the cake onto a serving plate.

Just before serving, using a fine-mesh sieve, dust the cake with confectioners' sugar and drizzle with caramel sauce.

MAKES 8–10 SERVINGS

FOLDING

This process is used to combine two mixtures or ingredients of different densities, such as a heavy batter and whipped egg whites: Scoop a third of the whites onto the center of the batter. Using a large rubber spatula, sweep it down through the whites to the bottom of the bowl, then draw the spatula back up in a circular motion, bringing some batter with it. Rotate the bowl a quarter turn. Repeat, rotating the bowl after each fold, just until the whites are incorporated. Now that the batter is lightened, fold in the remaining egg whites.

7 oz (200 g) 70-percent bittersweet chocolate, finely chopped (page 36)

¾ cup (6 oz/170 g) unsalted butter, cut into chunks

1 cup (7 oz/200 g) superfine (caster) sugar

4 large eggs, separated, at room temperature

½ teaspoon almond extract (essence)

¼ cup (1 oz/30 g) plus 1 tablespoon cake (soft-wheat) flour

¼ teaspoon salt

½ cup (3 oz/85 g) lightly toasted blanched whole almonds (page 47)

Confectioners' (icing) sugar for dusting

Caramel Sauce (page 114), chilled, for serving

HAZELNUT DACQUOISES

1¾ cups (9½ oz/270 g)
hazelnuts (filberts),
toasted *(far right)*

2¼ cups (8 oz/225 g)
confectioners' (icing) sugar,
plus extra for dusting

3 large egg whites,
at room temperature

¼ cup (2 oz/60 g)
granulated sugar

⅔ cup (5 oz/140 g)
plus 1 tablespoon
unsalted butter, at
room temperature

2 tablespoons Cognac

Pastry Cream (page 113),
chilled

Preheat the oven to 300°F (150°C). On a piece of parchment (baking) paper, draw 16 circles, each 2½ inches (6 cm) in diameter and 1½ inches (4 cm) apart. Put the paper, marked side down, on a 12-by-18-by-1-inch (30-by-45-by-2.5-cm) baking sheet.

In a food processor, process ⅔ cup (3½ oz/100 g) of the hazelnuts and 1 cup (3½ oz/100 g) of the confectioners' sugar until finely ground. Using a stand mixer, beat the egg whites with the whisk on medium speed until they start to foam. Add a third of the granulated sugar and beat until the whites are opaque, then add another third of the sugar. When the whites start to become firm, add the remaining sugar and increase the speed to high. Beat until the whites form firm peaks but still look wet (page 14). Carefully fold in the ground hazelnut mixture in 2 additions. Fill a pastry bag fitted with a ⅜-inch (1-cm) plain tip with the mixture (page 98). Starting in the center of each circle, pipe a continuous spiral, filling the circles. Dust the meringue disks with confectioners' sugar. Bake until the disks are browned and firm, 45–50 minutes. Transfer the disks, still on the paper, to a wire rack.

Using the stand mixer, beat the butter with the paddle on medium speed until creamy. In a food processor, process ¾ cup (4 oz/110 g) of the hazelnuts and the remaining 1¼ cups (4½ oz/125 g) confectioners' sugar until finely ground. Add to the butter and beat until thick. Add the Cognac. Reduce the speed to medium-low and beat in the pastry cream in 4 additions.

Put half of the filling in a pastry bag fitted with a ⅜-inch (1-cm) plain tip. Pipe the mixture on top of 8 meringues, dividing it evenly. Press the remaining meringues on top. Freeze for 30 minutes. Using a spatula, cover the sides with the remaining filling. Chop the remaining ⅓ cup (2 oz/60 g) hazelnuts; spread on waxed paper. Roll each pastry in the nuts to coat the sides. Refrigerate until serving.

MAKES 8 SERVINGS

TOASTING HAZELNUTS

A light toasting heightens the flavor of nuts. Toasting hazelnuts also loosens their skins. Spread the nuts in a single layer on a baking sheet lined with parchment (baking) paper and toast in a preheated 350°F (180°C) oven until the skins start to darken and wrinkle, about 8 minutes. When the nuts are cool enough to handle, wrap them in a kitchen towel and rub vigorously to remove the skins. Not every speck will come off. Toast walnut halves and pieces and whole and sliced (flaked) almonds in the same way. Sliced almonds will take less time, however. Check them after 4 minutes.

CLOCHE CAFÉ

Preheat the oven to 350°F (180°C). Generously butter a 6-cup (48–fl oz/1.5-l) charlotte mold. Using a stand mixer, beat the egg whites with the whisk on medium speed until they start to foam. Add a third of the granulated sugar and beat until the whites are opaque, then add another third of the sugar. When the whites start to become firm and increase in volume, add the remaining sugar and increase the speed to high. Beat until the whites form soft peaks but still look wet (page 14). In another bowl, whisk the yolks by hand until blended. Using a large rubber spatula, carefully fold the yolks into the whites. Sift the flour over the egg mixture in 2 additions and carefully fold in.

Pour the batter into the prepared mold and smooth the top. Bake until the cake is browned and puffed, and a skewer inserted into the center comes out clean, 20–25 minutes. Let cool on a wire rack for 10 minutes, then unmold. If necessary, tap the pan on a counter to release the cake.

Cut the cake into 4 equal layers *(left)*. Put the widest layer, cut side up, on a serving plate. Brush with some of the coffee sugar syrup. Reserve about half of the buttercream for the outside of the cake. Spread a thin layer of the remaining buttercream on the layer. Continue to alternate layers of cake brushed with syrup and spread with buttercream. You will have 4 layers of cake and 3 layers of buttercream. The shape of the assembled cake will resemble that of the mold (and original whole baked cake). Refrigerate for 30 minutes. Spread the buttercream over the top and sides (page 111). Dust the cake with confectioners' sugar and decorate with candied coffee beans. Refrigerate until ready to serve.

Note: To make coffee sugar syrup, follow the instructions for making regular sugar syrup (page 55), but add 1 teaspoon instant espresso powder to the sugar before dissolving in the water.

MAKES 6–8 SERVINGS

CUTTING CAKE LAYERS
Toothpicks make excellent guides for cutting a cake into layers. Using a ruler, insert toothpicks at regular intervals around the side of the cake, dividing it into 2, 3, or even 4 horizontal layers. Placing one hand on top of the cake, and using a long, serrated knife positioned just above the line of toothpicks marking the layer, cut the cake with an even sawing motion. Lift off the top layer and carefully set it aside, then remove the row of toothpicks you used as a guide. If the cake has more than 2 layers, repeat to cut the additional layers.

5 large eggs, separated, plus 1 large egg yolk, at room temperature

⅔ cup (4½ oz/125 g) granulated sugar

1 cup (4½ oz/125 g) unbleached all-purpose (plain) flour

Coffee sugar syrup (see Note)

Coffee Meringue Buttercream (page 114)

Confectioners' (icing) sugar for dusting

Candied coffee beans for decorating

CHOCOLATE VACHERINS

1 cup (3½ oz/100 g) confectioners' (icing) sugar

¼ cup (1 oz/30 g) Dutch-process cocoa powder (page 13)

3 large egg whites, at room temperature

½ cup (3½ oz/100 g) granulated sugar

4 cups (32 fl oz/900 ml) orange, lemon, or raspberry sorbet or vanilla or coffee ice cream for serving

Preheat the oven to 300°F (150°C). On a piece of parchment (baking) paper large enough to fit on a 12-by-18-by-1-inch (30-by-45-by-2.5-cm) baking sheet, draw 8 circles, each 3 inches (7.5 cm) in diameter and 1 inch (2.5 cm) apart. Put the paper, marked side down, on the sheet.

Sift the confectioners' sugar and cocoa powder together onto a sheet of waxed paper; set aside.

Using a stand mixer, beat the egg whites with the whisk on medium speed until they start to foam. Add a third of the granulated sugar and beat until the whites are opaque, then add another third of the sugar. When the whites start to increase in volume and become firm, add the remaining sugar and increase the speed to high. Beat until the whites form soft peaks but still look wet (page 14). Remove the bowl from the mixer. Sift a third of the dry ingredients over the egg whites and carefully fold in with a large rubber spatula. Sift and fold in the remaining dry ingredients in 2 more additions.

Spoon the mixture into a pastry bag fitted with a ⅜-inch (1-cm) plain tip (page 98). Starting in the center of each circle, pipe a continuous spiral, filling the circles. Pipe another ring on top of the outer rim of each circle. Bake until the meringues are firm and one can be lifted from the paper, about 1 hour. Transfer the meringues, still on the paper, to a wire rack and let cool completely.

Store the meringues in an airtight container for up to 2 weeks until ready to fill and serve. If the meringues become soggy, crisp them in a 200°F (95°C) oven for 30–40 minutes. To serve, fill each meringue with a scoop of sorbet or ice cream.

MAKES 8 SERVINGS

VACHERINS

Vacherins are disk-shaped cow's milk cheeses produced in Switzerland and France. Dessert vacherins, fashioned from meringue, are likely so named because they have the same shape. Large versions are made by piping a round of meringue for the base and a series of rings for the sides, baking them all until dry, then stacking the rings onto the base, sealing them with meringue, and baking them again. For individual vacherins, a single ring is piped onto the base and the cups are baked once. Both sizes are filled with sorbet, ice cream, fruit, or whipped cream.

ROLLED CHESTNUT CREAM CAKE

CHESTNUT PURÉE

Canned chestnut purée comes in a variety of guises. It can be plain, seasoned with a little salt for use in savory preparations, or sweetened. For this cake, look for sweetened purée laced with crumbled bits of candied chestnuts. It is often labeled "chestnut spread." The spread is regularly used in the making of tortes, as a topping for ice cream, and as filling for pastries. It is also passed through a ricer and topped with whipped cream to make the classic French dessert known as Mont Blanc. Chestnut spread is carried in well-stocked grocery stores.

Preheat the oven to 475°F (245°C). Line a 12-by-18-by-1-inch (30-by-45-by-2.5-cm) baking sheet with parchment (baking) paper and butter the sides. Sift the flour and cocoa powder together onto a sheet of waxed paper; set aside. Put the egg yolks and the whole eggs in the bowl of a stand mixer. Beat with the whisk on medium speed while adding the ⅓ cup sugar in a steady stream. Increase the speed to high and beat until the eggs are almost doubled in volume, about 5 minutes. Transfer to a large bowl.

Thoroughly wash and dry the mixer bowl and whisk. Use the stand mixer to beat the egg whites with the whisk on medium speed until they start to foam. Add a third of the 1 tablespoon sugar and beat until opaque, then add another third of the sugar. When the whites start to increase in volume, add the remaining sugar and increase the speed to high. Beat until the whites form soft peaks but still look wet (page 14). Fold the whites into the egg yolk mixture. Sift the dry ingredients over the egg mixture and fold in.

Pour the batter onto the prepared sheet and spread evenly. Bake until the cake is springy to the touch, 5–8 minutes, rotating the sheet halfway through. Run a table knife around the edge and slide the cake, still on the paper, onto a wire rack. Let cool completely.

Whip the cream to soft peaks (page 80). Carefully fold in the chestnut spread. Place the cake, paper side up, on another piece of parchment paper. Peel off the top piece of paper. Spread with about a third of the whipped cream mixture. Sprinkle with the chopped chocolate. With a long side of the cake toward you, roll it into a log (page 71). Transfer, seam side down, to a serving plate. Put the remaining whipped cream mixture into a pastry bag fitted with a ¾-inch (2-cm) star tip. Starting where the log meets the plate, pipe lines of cream onto the log from end to end (page 98). Decorate with chocolate curls. Refrigerate until ready to serve.

MAKES 14–16 SERVINGS

¼ cup (1 oz/30 g) cake (soft-wheat) flour

2 tablespoons Dutch-process cocoa powder (page 13)

2 large eggs, separated, plus 2 whole large eggs, at room temperature

⅓ cup (2½ oz/70 g) plus 1 tablespoon sugar

2 cups (16 fl oz/450 ml) heavy (double) cream

¾ cup (9 oz/250 g) sweetened chestnut purée *(far left)*

3 oz (85 g) bittersweet chocolate, finely chopped (page 36)

Chocolate curls or large chocolate petals for decorating (page 102)

HAZELNUT CAKE WITH CHOCOLATE GLAZE

GANACHE

A marriage of chocolate and heavy (double) cream, ganache can be used for filling or icing a cake. The proportions of the two ingredients can vary, and sometimes butter and/or liquor are added. Equal parts of chocolate and cream by weight are typically used for making a filling; the cream is heated and poured over chopped chocolate, then the two are whisked together and allowed to cool. A ganache icing, which calls for more cream than chocolate, is heated and then allowed to cool to barely lukewarm, for a spreadable finish.

Preheat the oven to 325°F (165°C). Line the bottom of a 12-by-18-by-1-inch (30-by-45-by-2.5-cm) baking sheet with parchment (baking) paper.

Sift the flour, cocoa powder, and salt together onto a sheet of waxed paper. Stir in the hazelnuts. Set aside.

Using a stand mixer, beat the egg yolks and 1 cup (7 oz/200 g) of the sugar with the whisk on medium-high speed until the mixture is pale and thick, 3–5 minutes. Transfer to a large bowl.

Thoroughly wash and dry the mixer bowl and whisk. Beat the egg whites with the whisk on medium speed until they start to foam. Add a third of the remaining ¼ cup (2 oz/50 g) sugar and beat until the whites are opaque, then add another third of the sugar. When the whites start to increase in volume and become firm, add the remaining sugar and increase the speed to high. Beat until the whites form soft peaks but still look wet (page 14).

Using a large rubber spatula, carefully fold the dry ingredients into the yolk mixture. The batter will be very thick. Fold in the melted butter in 2 additions. Using the spatula, fold a third of the whites into the batter, then fold in the remaining whites.

Pour the batter onto the prepared sheet and, using an offset frosting spatula, spread it as evenly as possible. Bake until the cake is puffed and springy to the touch, 10–15 minutes. Let cool completely on a wire rack.

(Continued on next page.)

1 cup (4½ oz/125 g) unbleached all-purpose (plain) flour

½ cup (2 oz/60 g) Dutch-process cocoa powder (page 13)

¼ teaspoon salt

⅔ cup (3½ oz/100 g) hazelnuts (filberts), lightly toasted (page 47) and finely chopped

9 large eggs, separated, at room temperature

1¼ cups (9 oz/250 g) sugar

½ cup (4 oz/110 g) unsalted butter, melted and cooled to room temperature

FOR THE GLAZE AND FINISH:

12 oz (335 g) bittersweet chocolate, finely chopped (page 36)

1½ cups (12 fl oz/335 ml) heavy (double) cream

1 teaspoon dark rum

Sugar syrup *(far right)*

2 oz (60 g) semisweet (plain) or bittersweet chocolate, finely chopped

8–12 candied flowers (page 105)

Meanwhile, make the glaze and finish: Place the bittersweet chocolate into a bowl. In a small saucepan over medium heat, heat the cream until small bubbles appear along the edge of the pan, then pour it over the chocolate. Gently whisk together by hand until the chocolate is melted, to make a ganache *(far left)*. Let cool to the consistency of stiff mayonnaise.

Put a piece of parchment paper on a work surface. Run a table knife around the edge of the pan. Holding a long side of the cake, invert the pan onto the paper. Remove the pan and peel off the top paper. Cut the cake into three 12-by-5-inch (30-by-13-cm) rectangles. Put one of the rectangles on a serving platter.

In a small bowl, combine the rum and sugar syrup. Brush the cake with some of the syrup. Spread with about a fourth of the ganache. Position another piece of cake on the ganache. Brush with some of the syrup. Spread another fourth of the ganache on top. Position the third piece of cake on the ganache and brush with the remaining syrup. Refrigerate the cake for 30 minutes to firm the filling.

Using a serrated knife, trim the edges of the cake. Place the remaining ganache in a bowl and place over a saucepan of simmering water, stirring occasionally, until the ganache is soft enough to spread. Using a small offset frosting spatula, spread the ganache on the top and sides of the cake, making it as smooth as possible. Melt the semisweet chocolate and use a parchment paper cone to pipe a decorative lace pattern on the top of the cake (page 101). Decorate the cake with the candied flowers. Refrigerate until ready to serve. To serve, cut into slices with a thin, sharp knife.

MAKES 12–14 SERVINGS

(Photograph appears on following page.)

SUGAR SYRUP

Dense cakes like this one, as well as génoise cakes (page 63), are made with a small amount of butter, which can produce a somewhat dry cake. Brushing a sugar syrup onto the layers as they are assembled helps keep them moist. To make the sugar syrup, combine ¼ cup (2 oz/60 g) sugar and ¼ cup (2 fl oz/60 ml) water in a small saucepan over medium heat. Bring to a boil, stirring occasionally until the sugar dissolves. Remove from the heat and let cool to room temperature. If a flavoring is indicated, stir it into the cooled syrup.

SPRING AND SUMMER CAKES

When the trees start to bud and the days grow long and warm, it is time for light, refreshing desserts. Take advantage of berries and other fresh fruits by pairing them with sponge cakes and billows of whipped cream. Or balance a rich buttercream with the tartness of lemon curd. When you want a touch of feathery sweetness, bake a chiffon cake.

LEMON SPONGE CAKE

Preheat the oven to 375°F (190°C). Line the bottom of a 9-by-3-inch (23-by-7.5-cm) round cake pan with parchment (baking) paper.

Using a stand mixer, beat the eggs and sugar with the whisk on high speed until tripled in volume, about 5 minutes. Beat in the lemon extract. Remove the bowl from the mixer. Sift the flour over the egg mixture in 2 additions and carefully fold in with a large rubber spatula. Fold a large dollop into the melted butter, then fold back into the egg mixture. Pour into the prepared pan and smooth the top. Bake until the cake is puffed, 20–25 minutes. Let cool completely on a wire rack.

Meanwhile, make the filling and frosting: Whip the cream to soft peaks (page 80). Put the lemon curd in a bowl and carefully fold in the whipped cream in 2 additions.

Run a table knife around the edge of the pan and unmold the cake onto a work surface. Turn right side up, leaving the parchment paper in place. Cut the cake into 2 equal layers (page 48). Put the top layer, cut side up, on a serving plate. Brush with some of the sugar syrup. Reserve a third of the buttercream for decorating the frosted cake. Fill a pastry bag fitted with a ½-inch (12-mm) plain tip with about ¾ cup (6 fl oz/170 ml) of the buttercream, and pipe a ring around the outside edge of the cake (page 98). Evenly spread the whipped cream mixture inside the buttercream ring. Position the second layer, cut side down, on the cream and peel off the paper. Brush with the remaining syrup. Refrigerate for 30 minutes; keep the remaining buttercream at room temperature.

Spread buttercream on the top and sides of the cake (page 111). Spoon the reserved buttercream into the pastry bag fitted with a ½-inch (12-mm) star tip and pipe shells around the top edge (page 98). Refrigerate until 30 minutes before serving.

MAKES 10–12 SERVINGS

CAKE FLOUR

Cake flour is milled from soft wheat and, as a result, contains less gluten and more starch than all-purpose (plain) flour. Because cake flour is milled finer than other flours, its particles are small, allowing it to blend into a batter easily. Cake flour is also bleached, which enables it to tolerate the high proportion of sugar and fat in cake batters. All these characteristics produce a tender cake with a fine crumb, making cake flour appropriate for this lemon sponge and other delicate cakes.

5 large eggs, at room temperature

¾ cup (5½ oz/155 g) sugar

¾ teaspoon lemon extract (essence)

1 cup (4 oz/110 g) cake (soft-wheat) flour, sifted

¼ cup (2 oz/60 g) unsalted butter, melted and cooled to room temperature

FOR THE FILLING
AND FROSTING:

½ cup (4 fl oz/110 ml) heavy (double) cream

Lemon Curd (page 115)

Sugar Syrup (page 55)

Lemon Buttercream (page 115)

STRAWBERRY GÉNOISE WITH WHIPPED CREAM

FOR THE GÉNOISE:

4 large eggs

½ cup (3½ oz/100 g) granulated sugar

¾ cup (3 oz/85 g) cake (soft-wheat) flour, sifted

3 tablespoons unsalted butter, melted

FOR THE FILLING
AND FINISH:

1 teaspoon kirsch

Sugar Syrup (page 55)

2 cups (16 fl oz/450 ml) heavy (double) cream

2 teaspoons confectioners' (icing) sugar

3 cups (12 oz/335 g) strawberries, hulled and cut into ½-inch (12-mm) slices, plus 6 strawberries, halved lengthwise, for garnish.

To make the génoise, preheat the oven to 375°F (190°C). Line the bottom of a 9-by-3-inch (23-by-7.5-cm) round cake pan with parchment (baking) paper.

In the bowl of a stand mixer, whisk together the eggs and granulated sugar by hand until combined. Place the bowl over a pan of simmering water. Gently whisk until the mixture registers 140°F (60°C) on an instant-read thermometer, about 3 minutes. Put the bowl on the mixer and beat with the whisk on high speed until the mixture is pale and almost tripled in volume, 5–8 minutes. Remove the bowl from the mixer. Sift the flour over the egg mixture in 2 additions and carefully fold in with a large rubber spatula. Fold a large dollop into the melted butter, then fold back into the egg mixture.

Pour into the prepared pan and smooth the top. Bake until the top is browned, about 20 minutes. Let cool completely on a wire rack. Run a table knife around the edge of the pan and invert the cake onto a work surface. Turn the cake right side up, leaving the parchment paper in place. Cut the cake into 2 equal layers (page 48). Put the top layer, cut side up, on a serving plate.

To make the filling and finish, in a small bowl, stir together the kirsch and sugar syrup. Whip the cream and confectioners' sugar to soft peaks (page 80). Place the sliced strawberries in a bowl. Fold about a fourth of the cream into the berries. Spread the mixture evenly on top of the cake. Position the remaining layer, cut side down, on top. Peel off the paper. Brush with the remaining syrup. Spread the top and sides of the cake with the remaining whipped cream (page 111). Thinly slice one strawberry half and place it in the center of the cake. Arrange the remaining halves around the edge of the cake. Refrigerate until ready to serve.

MAKES 8–10 SERVINGS

GÉNOISE

The génoise, a light, elegant sponge cake, is one of the building blocks of French baking, used as a base for both layer cakes and jelly rolls. The successful leavening of the cake depends solely on how much air is whipped into the eggs. Heating the sugar and whole eggs before whipping helps the eggs attain the maximum volume possible, although a slightly denser, still satisfying, version of the cake can be made without this step. Some génoises, such as this recipe, contain a little butter, which tenderizes the crumb.

ALMOND AND CHERRY CHEESECAKE

BISCOTTI CRUST

The Italian cookies known as biscotti, meaning "twice baked," have a crunchy texture perfect for creating a thin crumb crust. The almond-flavored variety called for here boosts the flavor of the almond extract and liqueur used in the cheesecake filling.

Before making the crust, butter the bottom and sides of the pan. In a food processor, process 4 almond biscotti (about 4 oz/110 g) to a fine powder. Transfer to a bowl. Add 2 tablespoons melted unsalted butter and mix until evenly combined. Place in the prepared pan and spread in an even layer over the bottom.

To make the cheesecake, in a large frying pan over medium-high heat, melt the butter. Add the cherries and 1 tablespoon of the lemon juice and cook for about 1 minute. Sprinkle with the ¼ cup sugar and cook, stirring, for 3–5 minutes. Stir in the amaretto and cook for 1 minute. Refrigerate until completely cool.

Preheat the oven to 300°F (150°C). Completely wrap the outside of a 9-inch (23-cm) springform pan (page 112) with a double thickness of wide aluminum foil. Make the biscotti crust.

Using a stand mixer, beat the cream cheese and 1¼ cups sugar with the paddle on medium-high speed until smooth. Beat in the cornstarch. Add the eggs one at a time, beating until incorporated. Beat in the sour cream, remaining 1 tablespoon lemon juice, vanilla and almond extracts, and salt. Pour the cherry mixture into the pan and spread it evenly, without marring the crumb layer. Pour in the filling and spread it to the pan edges.

Set the pan inside a large roasting pan and fill with about 1 inch (2.5 cm) of very hot tap water. Bake for 1 hour. Turn off the oven and let the cheesecake cook in the warm oven, without opening the door, for 1 hour longer. Remove from the water bath and place on a wire rack.

To make the topping, lightly toast the almonds (page 47), then reduce the oven temperature to 300°F (150°C). In a bowl, whisk together the sour cream, sugar, and vanilla and almond extracts. Spread the topping over the warm cheesecake. Sprinkle with the almonds. Bake until the topping looks slightly set, about 8 minutes. Let cool for about 1 hour. Refrigerate for at least 8 hours or up to overnight. Remove the pan sides. Place the cake, on the pan bottom, on a serving plate and refrigerate until serving.

MAKES 12–14 SERVINGS

FOR THE CHEESECAKE:

2 tablespoons unsalted butter

3 cups (18 oz/500 g) fresh, frozen, or drained jarred Bing or other dark sweet cherries

2 tablespoons fresh lemon juice

1¼ cups (9 oz/250 g) plus ¼ cup (2 oz/60 g) sugar

2 tablespoons amaretto

Biscotti Crust (far left)

1½ lbs (670 g) cream cheese

1 tablespoon cornstarch (cornflour)

4 large eggs, at room temperature

1 cup (8 oz/225 g) sour cream

1 teaspoon each vanilla extract and almond extract (essence)

¼ teaspoon salt

FOR THE TOPPING:

¼ cup (1½ oz/45 g) sliced (flaked) almonds

1 cup (8 oz/225 g) sour cream

¼ cup (2 oz/60 g) sugar

1 teaspoon each vanilla extract and almond extract

RASPBERRY CHARLOTTE

Ladyfingers (page 113)

2¼ teaspoons (1 envelope) unflavored gelatin *(far right)*

¼ cup (2 fl oz/60 ml) water, plus 2 tablespoons cold water

½ cup (3½ oz/100 g) granulated sugar

6 cups (18 oz/500 g) raspberries

2 cups (16 fl oz/450 ml) heavy (double) cream

2 teaspoons confectioners' (icing) sugar

Make the ladyfingers and 2 cake rounds as directed. Place the small round in the bottom of an 8-cup (64–fl oz/1.8-l) charlotte mold with the rounded side down. Line the sides with the most attractive ladyfingers, with the rounded sides facing the mold.

In a small bowl, sprinkle the gelatin over the 2 tablespoons cold water, stir, and let soften until opaque, about 3 minutes. In a small saucepan over medium heat, combine the ¼ cup water and the granulated sugar and heat until the sugar dissolves, then stir in the softened gelatin. Using a fine-mesh sieve, strain the mixture into a bowl and let cool to room temperature. In a food processor or blender, purée 4 cups (12 oz/335 g) of the raspberries. You should have about 1½ cups (12 fl oz/335 ml) purée. Stir the purée into the gelatin mixture.

Whip 1¼ cups (10 fl oz/280 ml) of the cream to medium-stiff peaks (page 80). Using a large rubber spatula, stir a fourth of the cream into the raspberry purée, then carefully fold in the remaining cream. Fill the lined mold halfway with the raspberry cream. Cover the cream with a layer of ladyfingers, trimming them to fit if needed. Fill the mold with the remaining raspberry cream. Put the large round, rounded side down, on top the cream and inside the ladyfingers lining the mold. Refrigerate for at least 4 hours, or up to overnight.

Invert the mold onto a serving plate and lift off. Combine the remaining ¾ cup (6 fl oz/170 ml) cream and the confectioners' sugar and whip to medium peaks (page 80). Spoon the whipped cream into a pastry bag fitted with a ⅜-inch (1-cm) star tip, and pipe rosettes on top of the charlotte (page 98). Garnish with the remaining whole berries. Refrigerate the charlotte until serving.

MAKES 6–8 SERVINGS

GELATIN

This flavorless and colorless ingredient made from animal protein is sold in two forms, fine granules and sheets. Bakers rely on its unique properties to transform a liquid into a smooth jelled solid. Working with gelatin is easy. First, soften it, without stirring, in a little cold liquid, then stir the softened gelatin thoroughly into the liquid to be jelled and heat it gently without allowing it to boil. When cooled, the mixture will set into a firm mass. Use 2¼ teaspoons granules (1 envelope) or 4 gelatin sheets to jell 2–3 cups (16–24 fl oz/ 450–670 ml) liquid.

CHIFFON CAKE WITH SUMMER FRUIT COMPOTE

CHIFFON CAKE

Light and moist, chiffon cakes are an American invention of the late 1940s. The most noteworthy characteristic is the use of a flavorless oil, rather than butter. The oil, along with egg yolks, ensures a tender crumb, and whipped egg whites, aided by baking powder, deliver the height.

Because the oil is bland (grapeseed, shown above, and canola are good choices), other flavorings, such as citrus and vanilla, are always added. The batter is fairly liquid, so the egg whites must be whipped a little stiffer than for most baking recipes.

Preheat the oven to 325°F (165°C). Have ready an ungreased angel food cake pan 10 inches (25 cm) in diameter and 4 inches (10 cm) deep. Sift the flour, baking powder, and salt together into a large bowl. Add 1 cup (7 oz/200 g) of the granulated sugar. Add the egg yolks, water, oil, orange zest, and vanilla and whisk until smooth.

Using a stand mixer, beat the egg whites with the whisk on medium speed until they start to foam. Add a third of the remaining ½ cup (3½ oz/100 g) granulated sugar and beat until the whites are opaque, then add another third of the sugar. When the whites start to increase in volume, add the remaining sugar and increase the speed to high. Beat until the whites form firm peaks but still look wet (page 14). Using a large rubber spatula, carefully fold a third of the beaten whites into the batter, then fold in the remaining whites.

Pour the batter into the pan. Bake until puffed and lightly browned, 55–65 minutes. Immediately invert the cake onto a countertop if the pan has feet or, if it does not, over the neck of a wine bottle. Let cool completely. Run a thin-bladed knife around the outer sides of the pan and around the inside of the tube. Invert the cake onto a serving plate.

To make the glaze, in a bowl, whisk together the orange juice and confectioners' sugar. Pour over the cake and let run down the sides. Let the glaze set. To make the compote, put the fruit into a bowl, sprinkle with granulated sugar to taste, and gently stir.

To serve, spoon some of the compote alongside each slice.

Note: For the compote, use a combination of fruits in season: blueberries and/or halved strawberries with sliced nectarines, or sliced peeled peaches, or sliced plums.

MAKES 10–12 SERVINGS

2 cups (8 oz/225 g) cake (soft-wheat) flour

2½ teaspoons baking powder

¾ teaspoon salt

1½ cups (10½ oz/300 g) granulated sugar

6 large eggs, separated, plus 2 large egg whites, at room temperature

¾ cup (6 fl oz/170 ml) water

½ cup (4 fl oz/110 ml) canola oil

1 tablespoon grated orange zest (page 88)

1 tablespoon vanilla extract (essence)

FOR THE GLAZE:

3 tablespoons fresh orange juice

2 cups (7 oz/200 g) confectioners' (icing) sugar, sifted

FOR THE FRUIT COMPOTE:

2 cups (8 oz/225 g) mixed ripe fruit (see Note)

¼–½ cup (2–3½ oz/ 60–100 g) granulated sugar

ROLLED CAKE WITH MIXED BERRIES

2 large eggs, separated,
plus 2 whole large eggs,
at room temperature

⅓ cup (2½ oz/70 g) plus
1 tablespoon granulated
sugar

¼ cup (1 oz/30 g) cake
(soft-wheat) flour, sifted

FOR THE FILLING
AND FINISH:

1¾ cups (14 fl oz/390 ml)
heavy (double) cream

¾ cup (6 oz/170 g)
crème fraîche

1 cup (4 oz/110 g)
mixed berries, such
as whole raspberries,
blackberries, or
blueberries, or sliced
strawberries, plus
15 whole or sliced
berries for garnish

1 tablespoon
confectioners' (icing)
sugar

Preheat the oven to 475°F (245°C). Line a 12-by-18-by-1-inch (30-by-45-by-2.5 cm) baking sheet with parchment (baking) paper and butter the sides.

Using a stand mixer, beat the egg yolks and the whole eggs with the whisk on medium speed while adding the ⅓ cup granulated sugar in a steady stream. Increase the speed to high and beat until the eggs are almost doubled in volume, about 5 minutes. Transfer the egg mixture to a large bowl.

Thoroughly wash and dry the mixer bowl and whisk. Beat the egg whites with the whisk on medium speed until they start to foam. Add a third of the 1 tablespoon granulated sugar and beat until opaque, then add another third of the sugar. When the whites start to increase in volume, add the remaining sugar and increase the speed to high. Beat until the whites form soft peaks but still look wet (page 14). Carefully fold the whites into the egg yolk mixture. Sift the flour over the egg mixture and fold in. Pour onto the prepared sheet and spread as evenly as possible. Bake until the cake is springy to the touch, 5–8 minutes, rotating the pan halfway through. Run a table knife around the edge and slide the cake, still on the paper, onto a wire rack. Let cool completely.

Meanwhile, make the filling and finish: Whip ¾ cup (6 fl oz/170 ml) of the cream and the crème fraîche to soft peaks (page 80). Gently fold in the 1 cup berries. Place the cake, paper side up, on another piece of parchment paper. Peel off the top paper. Spread the whipped cream mixture on the cake. Roll it into a log *(right)*. Transfer, seam side down, to a serving plate. Whip the remaining 1 cup (8 fl oz/220 ml) cream and the confectioners' sugar to soft peaks. Spoon into a pastry bag fitted with a ¾-inch (2-cm) star tip, and pipe a spiral down the center of the cake (page 98). Garnish with the remaining berries. Refrigerate until ready to serve.

MAKES 14–16 SERVINGS

ROLLING A CAKE

For ease of rolling, always smooth the batter as evenly as possible in the pan and then bake the cake until lightly browned, but not dry. Once the cake has cooled, place it, still attached to the parchment paper, on a second piece of parchment, cake side down, and peel off the parchment. Spread the filling evenly over the cake. With a long side toward you, roll the edge of the cake onto itself, moving your hands carefully from one end of the side to the other to keep the roll even. Using both hands, continue to roll the cake into a cylinder.

MANGO LAYER CAKE WITH COCONUT AND BUTTERCREAM

PREPARING MANGO

Ripe mangoes give slightly when pressed and are highly fragrant at their stem end. To remove the fruit in cubes, stand the mango on a narrow side, with the stem end facing you. Using a sharp knife, cut down the length of the fruit, about 1 inch (2.5 cm) from the stem and just grazing the large, flat pit. Repeat on the other side of the pit. Score the cut side of each mango half in a grid pattern, stopping just short of the skin. Push against the skin side to pop the cubes out, then cut across the base of the cubes to free them.

Make the génoise as directed, let cool completely, and place right side up on a work surface. Carefully cut the cake into 2 equal layers (page 48). Put the top layer, cut side up, on a serving plate. In a small bowl, stir together the rum and sugar syrup. Brush the cake with about half of the syrup.

Spoon about a fourth of the buttercream into a pastry bag fitted with a ½-inch (12-mm) plain tip. Pipe a ring of buttercream around the outside edge of the cake (page 98). Evenly arrange the chopped mango inside the middle of the buttercream ring. Position the remaining layer, cut side down, on top. Peel off the parchment paper. Brush with the remaining syrup. Refrigerate the cake for 30 minutes to firm the filling; keep the remaining buttercream at room temperature.

Using a straight frosting spatula, spread the top and sides of the cake with the buttercream, making it as smooth as possible (page 111). Gently press some of the coconut onto the sides of the cake and sprinkle the rest on top. Refrigerate the cake until 30 minutes before serving to set the frosting.

MAKES 8–10 SERVINGS

Génoise (page 63)

1 teaspoon dark rum

Sugar Syrup (page 55)

Vanilla Buttercream (page 115)

1 large ripe mango, cubed and coarsely chopped *(far left)* (about 1½ cups/ 9 oz/250 g)

⅔ cup (2 oz/60 g) unsweetened shredded coconut, lightly toasted (page 18)

AUTUMN AND WINTER CAKES

The cold months are times for rich, satisfying desserts. Pears, dried fruits, preserves, and nuts are the foundation for these cakes, from a pear-topped gingerbread for Thanksgiving to an elegant Eggnog Bavarian Cream Cake to ring in the New Year. And be sure to have a Date-Walnut Loaf on hand to serve to friends who drop by during this festive season.

DATE-WALNUT LOAF

Preheat the oven to 325°F (165°C). Generously butter an 8½-by-4½-inch (21.5-by-11.5-cm) loaf pan. In a small bowl, soak the dates in 1 tablespoon of the brandy for about 10 minutes.

In a large bowl, using a large rubber spatula, stir together the dates, walnuts, baking soda, salt, melted butter, and water until combined. Mix in the sugar and eggs, then the flour.

Pour the batter into the prepared pan and bake until the cake is puffed and browned, and a skewer inserted into the center comes out clean, 50–60 minutes. Let cool completely on a wire rack.

Run a table knife around the edge of the pan and turn the cake out onto a serving plate. Turn it right side up. Spoon the remaining 2 tablespoons brandy, a little at a time, over the cake so that the cake absorbs all of it.

Note: This sturdy cake is ideal for shipping as a gift. The brandy not only adds flavor but also helps preserve the cake.

Serving Tip: Serve with afternoon coffee or tea or as a simple dessert.

MAKES 8–10 SERVINGS

DATES

Since ancient times, dates have been a staple of the Middle Eastern pantry. At least three dozen distinct varieties of date palm are cultivated. Because of their naturally tacky consistency and high sugar content, many people believe dates are a dried fruit. Although you can purchase dried dates, nearly all dates are sold in their fresh, soft, or semidry state *(above)*. Among the most popular types found in American and European markets are the moderately sweet Deglet Noor, a good choice for this recipe, and the rich, meaty Medjool. Buy dates pitted to eliminate a preparation step.

1 cup (5 oz/140 g) pitted dates, roughly chopped *(far left)*

3 tablespoons brandy or Grand Marnier

1 cup (3½ oz/100 g) walnuts, lightly toasted (page 47) and coarsely chopped

1½ teaspoons baking soda (bicarbonate of soda)

¼ teaspoon salt

3 tablespoons unsalted butter, melted and cooled to room temperature

¾ cup (6 fl oz/170 ml) warm water

¾ cup (5½ oz/155 g) sugar

2 large eggs, lightly beaten

1½ cups (7 oz/200 g) unbleached all-purpose (plain) flour

CARAMELIZED PEAR UPSIDE-DOWN GINGERBREAD

8 tablespoons (4 oz/110 g) unsalted butter, at room temperature

½ cup (3½ oz/100 g) granulated sugar

2 firm but ripe, large pears, such as Comice or Anjou, peeled, cored, and cut lengthwise into ⅛-inch (3-mm) slices

1¾ cups (8 oz/225 g) unbleached all-purpose (plain) flour

1½ teaspoons baking soda (bicarbonate of soda)

2 teaspoons ground ginger

½ teaspoon *each* ground cardamom and ground cinnamon

¼ teaspoon salt

1 tablespoon peeled and finely chopped fresh ginger

⅓ cup (2 oz/60 g) firmly packed dark brown sugar

1 large egg, at room temperature, lightly beaten

¾ cup (8 oz/225 g) light molasses

¾ cup (6 fl oz/170 ml) whole milk, at room temperature

In an 8-inch (20-cm) square, heavy aluminum cake pan placed over medium heat, melt 2 tablespoons of the butter. Add the granulated sugar and cook, stirring occasionally, until the sugar melts and turns light brown, 5–7 minutes. Arrange the pear slices in the pan in 4 overlapping rows. Set aside.

Preheat the oven to 350°F (180°C). Sift the flour, baking soda, ground ginger, cardamom, cinnamon, and salt together onto a sheet of waxed paper. Stir in the fresh ginger. Set aside.

Using a stand mixer, beat the remaining 6 tablespoons (3 oz/85 g) butter with the paddle on medium speed until creamy. Add the brown sugar and beat until the mixture is pale and fluffy. Slowly drizzle in the egg, beating each addition until incorporated before continuing (page 10). Beat in the molasses. Reduce the speed to medium-low and add the dry ingredients in 3 additions alternately with the milk in 2 additions, starting and ending with the dry ingredients. Beat just until combined. Pour the batter on top of the pears and spread it evenly to the edge of the pan. Bake until the top of the cake is puffed, 35–40 minutes. Let cool on a wire rack for 10 minutes.

Run a table knife around the edge of the pan and shake it to make sure the cake is not sticking. (If it is, set the pan over low heat and heat for 1–2 minutes, gently shaking it until the cake is free.) Place a serving plate upside down on the pan. Wearing oven mitts, invert the plate and pan together. Lift off the pan. Dislodge any pear slices that stick to the pan and arrange on top of the cake. Serve at room temperature.

MAKES 9 SERVINGS

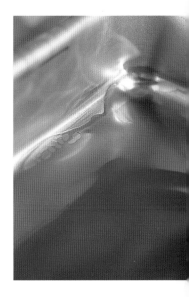

CARAMELIZING SUGAR

Sugar is usually caramelized in one of two ways: it is sprinkled in a heavy pan and cooked over low heat until it dissolves, then the heat is increased to medium, or it is dissolved in a little water over medium-high heat, forming a thick syrup. In both cases it is heated until it turns a rich brown. In this recipe, however, the sugar is mixed with butter for flavor. Rather than letting the sugar cook undisturbed to prevent crystallization, the butter-sugar mixture is stirred occasionally until it becomes light brown.

PECAN TORTE WITH BOURBON WHIPPED CREAM

WHIPPING CREAM

Beating air into cream stiffens it for use as a filling, frosting, or garnish. Always take cream for whipping straight from the refrigerator; cream allowed to stand at room temperature is more likely to separate as it is being whipped. Also chill the bowl and beaters (or whisk) on warm days or in a warm kitchen. If you have overwhipped the cream, and it is too stiff, try folding in a few tablespoons of cream, one at a time, from the carton. Keep in mind that cream labeled "ultrapasteurized" will not rise to the same billowing heights as regular pasteurized cream.

Preheat the oven to 325°F (165°C). Line the bottom of a 9-by-3-inch (23-by-7.5-cm) round cake pan with parchment (baking) paper. In a food processor, process the pecans, flour, and salt until finely ground; do not overprocess. Set aside.

Using a stand mixer, beat the egg yolks and ⅓ cup (2¼ oz/65 g) of the granulated sugar with the whisk on medium-high speed until pale and thick, 3–5 minutes. Using a large rubber spatula, fold in the pecan mixture. Transfer to a large bowl.

Thoroughly wash and dry the mixer bowl and whisk. Beat the egg whites with the whisk on medium speed until they start to foam. Add a third of the remaining ⅓ cup (2¼ oz/65 g) granulated sugar and beat until the whites are opaque, then add another third of the sugar. When the whites start to increase in volume and become firm, add the remaining sugar and increase the speed to high. Beat until the whites form soft peaks but still look wet (page 14). Using the spatula, carefully fold a third of the whites into the pecan mixture, then fold in the remaining whites.

Pour the batter into the prepared pan and smooth the top. Bake until lightly browned and a skewer inserted into the center comes out clean, 35–40 minutes. Let cool completely on a wire rack. Run a table knife around the edge of the pan and invert the torte onto a serving plate. Peel off the parchment paper. Put it right side up on the serving plate.

Just before serving, make the whipped cream: Whip the cream, confectioners' sugar, bourbon, and vanilla until the cream just holds its shape *(left)*. Cut the torte into wedges and place a dollop of whipped cream alongside each serving.

MAKES 10-12 SERVINGS

1¾ cups (7 oz/200 g) pecans

2 tablespoons unbleached all-purpose (plain) flour

¼ teaspoon salt

6 large eggs, separated, at room temperature

⅔ cup (4½ oz/130 g) granulated sugar

FOR THE WHIPPED CREAM:

½ cup (4 fl oz/110 ml) heavy (double) cream

1 teaspoon confectioners' (icing) sugar

2 teaspoons bourbon

1 teaspoon vanilla extract (essence)

BABAS AU RHUM

¼ cup (2 oz/60 g)
unsalted butter, at room
temperature

6 tablespoons (3 fl oz/
85 ml) whole milk,
warmed to 100°F (38°C)

2¼ teaspoons active
dry yeast

2 large eggs, at room
temperature, lightly beaten

1¾ cups (8 oz/225 g)
unbleached all-purpose
(plain) flour, plus flour
as needed

1 teaspoon salt

2 tablespoons sugar

FOR THE SYRUP:

1 cup (8 fl oz/225 ml)
water

½ cup (3½ oz/100 g) sugar

¼ cup (2 fl oz/60 ml)
dark rum

Vanilla ice cream or
sweetened whipped cream
(page 80) for serving

In a bowl, whisk the butter until creamy. Set aside.

Put the warm milk in the bowl of a stand mixer, sprinkle the yeast on top, and stir a few times. Let stand until the yeast dissolves. Add the eggs. Add the 1¾ cups flour, salt, and sugar and beat with the paddle on medium-low speed for 1 minute. Let the dough rest for 10 minutes. Switch to the dough hook and knead on medium speed for 3 minutes. Continuing to knead with the dough hook, add the whisked butter in 2 additions along with a scant 1 table-spoon flour to help the butter blend into the dough. Make sure the butter is incorporated before mixing in the second addition. Cover and let stand in a warm place until the dough doubles in bulk, 1½–2 hours.

Lightly butter 12 small 2-by-1¼-by-1¾-inch (5-by-3-by-4.5-cm) popover molds. Divide the dough among the molds, filling each about one-third full. Place on a baking sheet, then in a large plastic bag. Gently shake the bag a few times to incorporate air and tie the opening shut. Put the molds in a warm place until the dough rises enough to reach the top of the molds, 30–45 minutes. When the dough is almost ready, preheat the oven to 375°F (190°C).

Bake until the babas are browned and puffed, and pull away from the sides of the molds, 15–20 minutes. Let stand on a wire rack. The babas should be warm when soaked in the syrup.

Meanwhile, make the syrup: In a saucepan over medium heat, bring the water and sugar to a boil, stirring to dissolve the sugar. Let cool to lukewarm and add the rum. Pour into a shallow pan.

Soak the babas in the syrup, turning them frequently, until spongy but not falling apart, about 30 minutes. Transfer to dessert plates and serve with ice cream.

MAKES 12 SERVINGS

BABAS AU RHUM

Although theories about their history abound, these tall, cylindrical yeast-raised cakes probably originated in Russia and Poland, with the notion of a rum-based syrup added later by a Parisian pâtisserie. The height of a baba is the result of using yeast in the dough. Active dry yeast, one of the most convenient forms of yeast to use in baking, must first be dissolved in warm liquid before mixing with the other dough ingredients, causing both the natural sugars in the flour and the sugar in the dough to ferment. This action produces carbon dioxide, which makes the dough rise.

PUMPKIN MOUSSE CAKE

FRESH PUMPKIN PURÉE
To make fresh purée, choose a firm-fleshed cooking pumpkin. (Avoid large field pumpkins used for jack-o'-lanterns, as they are too watery.) Cut in half through the stem end and place, cut sides down, on a baking pan lined with parchment (baking) paper. Bake in a preheated 350°F (180°C) oven until a skewer pierces the flesh, about 25 minutes. Scoop out the seeds, scrape the flesh from the skin, and purée in a food processor. The purée should be the consistency of canned pumpkin. If it is too thin, cook over low heat until thickened. Freeze leftover purée for up to 3 months.

Make the génoise as directed, let cool completely, and place right side up on a work surface. Cut the cake into 2 equal layers (page 48).

In a small bowl, sprinkle the gelatin over the cold water, stir, and let soften until opaque, about 3 minutes. In a saucepan over medium heat, combine about ½ cup (4 oz/110 g) of the pumpkin purée, the granulated sugar, and the salt and heat, stirring, until the sugar dissolves. Stir in the softened gelatin and let cool to room temperature. In a bowl, stir the pumpkin mixture into the remaining pumpkin purée. Whisk in the cinnamon, cloves, nutmeg, and rum. Using a stand mixer or by hand, whip the 1⅔ cups cream to soft peaks (page 80). Using a large rubber spatula, gently fold a third of the cream into the purée, then fold in the remaining cream, making a mousse.

Peel off the paper from the bottom cake layer. Put the layer, cut side up, into the bottom of a 9-inch (23-cm) round springform pan. Spread half of the mousse evenly over the cake. Trim ½ inch (12 mm) from the outside edge of the remaining layer. Center it, cut side down, on top of the mousse. Top with the remaining mousse, pushing it between the cake and the pan and smoothing the top. Refrigerate until set, at least 4 hours, or up to overnight.

Warm the sides of the pan with a kitchen towel soaked in hot water and wrung out. Remove the pan sides and smooth the sides of the mousse with a frosting spatula. Whip the ½ cup cream and the confectioners' sugar to medium peaks (page 80). Spoon into a pastry bag fitted with a ½-inch (12-mm) star tip. Pipe shells around the top edge and a few in the center of the cake (page 98). Run a thin knife under the cake to free it from the bottom of the springform pan and transfer to a serving plate. Refrigerate until ready to serve.

MAKES 10–12 SERVINGS

Génoise (page 63)

2¼ teaspoons (1 envelope) unflavored gelatin (page 67)

2 tablespoons cold water

1¾ cups (15 oz/420 g) fresh pumpkin purée *(far left)* or canned pumpkin purée

½ cup (3½ oz/100 g) granulated sugar

¼ teaspoon salt

¼ teaspoon ground cinnamon

¼ teaspoon ground cloves

¼ teaspoon freshly grated nutmeg (page 17)

1 tablespoon dark rum

1⅔ cups (13 fl oz/360 ml) plus ½ cup (4 fl oz/110 ml) heavy (double) cream

1 teaspoon confectioners' (icing) sugar

EGGNOG BAVARIAN CREAM CAKE

Chocolate Ladyfingers
(page 113)

2¼ teaspoons (1 envelope)
unflavored gelatin
(page 67)

2 tablespoons cold water

1 cup (8 fl oz/225 ml)
whole milk

½ cup (4 oz/110 g) sugar

3 large egg yolks

2 teaspoons brandy or
Cognac

1 teaspoon vanilla extract
(essence)

⅛ teaspoon freshly grated
nutmeg (page 17)

1 cup (8 fl oz/225 ml)
heavy (double) cream

Chocolate curls for
decorating (page 102)

Make the ladyfingers as directed. Line a 5-cup (40–fl oz/1.1-l) brioche mold with the most attractive ladyfingers, trimming them to fit if needed and placing the rounded sides facing the mold.

In a small bowl, sprinkle the gelatin over the cold water, stir, and let soften until opaque, about 3 minutes. In a small saucepan over medium heat, heat the milk and ¼ cup (2 oz/55 g) of the sugar, stirring occasionally, until small bubbles appear along the edge of the pan.

Meanwhile, in a bowl, whisk together the egg yolks and the remaining ¼ cup (2 oz/55 g) sugar until well combined. Pour the hot milk mixture into the yolk mixture in a slow, steady stream, whisking constantly, then return the mixture to the pan. Cook over medium heat, whisking constantly, until the mixture thickens and registers 170°F (77°C) on an instant-read thermometer, 5–7 minutes. Remove from the heat and whisk in the softened gelatin. Using a fine-mesh sieve, strain the custard into a bowl. Stir in the brandy, vanilla, and nutmeg. Set the bowl in a larger bowl partially filled with ice water and whisk occasionally until the mixture cools and is just starting to set, about 10 minutes.

Meanwhile, whip the cream to soft peaks (page 80). Using a large rubber spatula, gently fold a third of the cream into the custard, then fold in the remaining cream. Pour the custard into the lined mold. Refrigerate until set, at least 4 hours.

Invert the mold onto a serving plate and warm the sides of the mold with a kitchen towel soaked in hot water and wrung out. Lift off the mold. Decorate the top with chocolate curls. Refrigerate until serving.

MAKES 8 SERVINGS

TEMPERING EGGS
If egg yolks are heated too quickly, they will curdle. To prevent this from happening when making the custard base for this Bavarian cream and similar recipes, you must "temper" the eggs, or heat them gently. First, pour hot milk in a thin stream into the yolks and sugar, whisking constantly. After returning this mixture to the saucepan over medium heat, whisk constantly to warm the eggs gradually and thicken the custard. Use an instant-read thermometer to test the temperature; it should not rise above 170°F (77°C) or the eggs will harden.

GÂTEAU BASQUE

Preheat the oven to 325°F (165°C). Line the bottom of a 9-by-3-inch (23-by-7.5-cm) round cake pan with parchment (baking) paper. Sift the flour, baking powder, and salt together onto a sheet of waxed paper; set aside. Remove the zest from the orange, then juice the orange *(left)*. You should have ⅓ cup (3 fl oz/80 ml) juice.

Using a stand mixer, beat 3 of the eggs and the sugar with the whisk on high speed until the mixture is pale, thick, and almost doubled in volume, 4–5 minutes. Reduce the speed to low. Beat in the orange zest and juice and vanilla. Increase the speed to medium-low and add the dry ingredients in 3 additions alternately with the melted butter in 2 additions, starting and ending with the dry ingredients, and drizzling the butter in slowly. Beat just until combined.

Pour half of the batter into the prepared pan, spreading it to the edges with a small offset frosting spatula. Spread the pastry cream on top, to within 1 inch (2.5 cm) of the sides of the pan, smoothing it with the spatula. Carefully spread the preserves over the pastry cream to within 1 inch (2.5 cm) of the pan sides. Pour the remaining batter on top, carefully spreading it to the edge of the pan and covering the pastry cream and preserves.

In a small bowl, whisk together the remaining egg with the water and gently brush the mixture on top of the cake. (There will be some left over.) Bake until the cake is puffed and nicely browned, 50–55 minutes. Let cool completely on a wire rack. Run a table knife around the edge of the pan and invert the cake onto a serving plate. Peel off the parchment paper and turn the cake right side up.

MAKES 8–10 SERVINGS

ZESTING AND JUICING CITRUS

A variety of tools are available for removing the zest, the colored portion of the peel, from citrus fruits. They include old-fashioned handheld graters with fine rasps, Microplane graters with razor-edged holes, zesters that remove fine strips in a single stroke, and paring knives or vegetable peelers for cutting away zest in long strips. When juicing only a few fruits, a simple hand device, such as a wooden reamer or a shallow bowl with a fluted, inverted cone at its center, will suffice. When you need both zest and juice, remove the zest first.

2 cups (9 oz/250 g) unbleached all-purpose (plain) flour

2 teaspoons baking powder

¼ teaspoon salt

1 medium orange

4 large eggs, at room temperature

1¼ cups (9 oz/250 g) sugar

2 teaspoons vanilla extract (essence)

¾ cup (6 oz/170 g) unsalted butter, melted and cooled to room temperature

Pastry Cream (page 113), chilled

¼ cup (2½ oz/70 g) cherry, raspberry, or strawberry preserves

1 tablespoon water

NESSELRODE CAKE

5 large eggs, at room temperature

¾ cup (5½ oz/155 g) sugar

1 cup (4 oz/110 g) cake (soft-wheat) flour, sifted

¼ cup (2 oz/60 g) unsalted butter, melted and cooled to room temperature

FOR THE FILLING AND FROSTING:

1 cup (8 fl oz/225 ml) heavy (double) cream

Pastry Cream (page 113), chilled

½ cup (3 oz/85 g) plus 2 tablespoons mixed dried fruit, such as dried currants, cranberries, and cherries, and chopped candied citrus zest (page 105)

½ cup (2½ oz/70 g) plus 2 tablespoons sliced (flaked) almonds, lightly toasted (page 47)

1 teaspoon Grand Marnier

Sugar Syrup (page 55)

Vanilla Buttercream (page 115)

6 candied chestnuts, thinly sliced (optional)

Preheat the oven to 375°F (190°C). Line the bottom of a 9-by-3-inch (23-by-7.5-cm) round cake pan with parchment (baking) paper.

Using a stand mixer, beat the eggs and sugar with the whisk on high speed until the mixture is tripled in volume, about 5 minutes. Remove the bowl from the mixer. Sift the flour over the egg mixture in 2 additions and carefully fold in with a large rubber spatula. Fold a large dollop into the melted butter, then fold back into the egg mixture. Pour into the prepared pan and smooth the top. Bake until the cake is puffed, 20–25 minutes. Let cool completely on a wire rack.

Meanwhile, make the filling and frosting: Whip the cream to soft peaks (page 80). Put the pastry cream in a bowl and then fold in the whipped cream in 2 additions. Fold in the ½ cup dried fruit and candied zest and the 2 tablespoons almonds. In a small bowl, stir together the Grand Marnier and sugar syrup.

Run a table knife around the edge of the pan and unmold the cake onto a work surface. Turn right side up, leaving the parchment paper in place. Cut the cake into 3 equal layers (page 48). Put the top layer, cut side up, on a serving plate. Brush the layer with some of the syrup. Spread half of the whipped cream mixture on top. Position the middle layer on the cream. Brush with some of the syrup and spread the remaining cream mixture on top. Position the third layer, cut side down, on the cream and peel off the paper. Brush with the remaining syrup. Refrigerate for 30 minutes.

Evenly spread the buttercream on the top and sides of the cake (page 111). Press the ½ cup almonds onto the sides. Arrange the 2 tablespoons dried fruit and candied zest and the chestnut slices (if using) in a ring around the top edge. Refrigerate until 30 minutes before serving to set the frosting.

MAKES 10–12 SERVINGS

NESSELRODE CAKE

The inspiration for this cake comes from Nesselrode pudding, a Russian dessert based on chestnuts, egg custard, dried fruits and candied zest, and cream. It was created in the early nineteenth century to honor Count Nesselrode, a leading figure in the drafting of the Holy Alliance of 1815, an agreement among the monarchs of Austria, Prussia, and Russia. Later, the pudding was included at one of the grand meals that novelist Marcel Proust describes in *Remembrance of Things Past*. Here, cake layers are filled with a rich mixture that recalls the legendary Russian dessert.

DECORATED CAKES

Any cake can be easily dressed up. Create a simple, elegant design with a dusting of confectioners' (icing) sugar or add texture to a plain frosted cake with a variety of easily mastered techniques. With a bit of practice, you can also learn the art of piping frosting, fashioning curls from chocolate, and candying flowers.

DECORATING WITH CONFECTIONERS' SUGAR AND COCOA

CAKE STENCILS
To make a stencil from parchment (baking) paper, cut out
a piece slightly larger than the
diameter of the cake. For ease,
draw relatively simple shapes
(circles, triangles, stars), or
trace around the outside of
small pastry cutters, spacing
the shapes generously. Cut out
the shapes with small, sharp
scissors, then lay the stencil on
top of the cake and dust with
confectioners' sugar or cocoa,
releasing a solid dusting on
the areas of the cake
exposed through the cutouts.
Lift the paper straight up to
prevent smudging.

For a very simple design, place a wire cooling rack on top of a cake. Put about ⅓ cup (1 oz/30 g) confectioners' sugar in a fine-mesh sieve and tap the sieve gently as you move it over the cake. If desired, cut wide strips of parchment (baking) paper and arrange them on top of the cake to make a simple pattern, such as a grid, then dust the cake with confectioners' sugar.

For a fancier design, cut a stencil out of parchment paper. Keep the design simple, as intricate patterns tend to blur. Lay the stencil on the cake and, using a fine-mesh sieve, dust with confectioners' sugar. Carefully remove the stencil.

For a two-tone design, use a fine-mesh sieve to sift confectioners' sugar over the top of the cake. Then set a small brioche mold or small tart pan on the center of the cake and lightly sift cocoa powder around it (see Almost Flourless Chocolate Torte, page 36). Or, sift cocoa over the top of the cake, then arrange strips of parchment paper on the cake to make a grid, dust the cake with confectioners' sugar, and carefully remove the strips *(opposite)*.

Note: Reusable cake stencils in myriad designs can be purchased in specialty shops and by mail order.

MAKES 1 DECORATED CAKE

1 undecorated cake
(page 36)

Confectioners' (icing) sugar
for dusting

Dutch-process cocoa
powder for dusting
(page 13)

TEXTURING FROSTING

1 frosted cake (page 10)

To make peaks on top of a frosted cake, touch the back of a serving teaspoon (not the measuring type) on the top of the frosted cake and pull it up in a quick jerking motion. Use this same technique with a tablespoon to create waves.

To make a crosshatch pattern on top of the cake, hold a fork upside down and at a slight angle to the top of the cake. Gently draw the tines of the fork through the frosting, making two or three passes so the top has bands of lines evenly interspersed with smooth bands. Rotate the cake 90 degrees and repeat.

To make wavy lines across the top of a cake, hold a decorating comb at a slight angle with the top extending beyond the edge of the cake. Lightly drag the comb in a wavy pattern across the cake. Wipe the comb with a paper towel. Align the comb with the last line in the pattern you just made, and drag it over the top again. Continue until the entire top of the cake is textured *(opposite)*. To decorate the side, hold the comb at a slight angle against the side and turn the cake with your other hand, making horizontal lines around the circumference.

MAKES 1 DECORATED CAKE

DECORATING COMBS

The most common decorating combs are metal or plastic triangles with teeth on each side that vary in number and length and sometimes shape. Plastic squares with rounded sides are also available, as are rectangular combs with teeth on one or two sides. Use the combs to make wavy, straight, or circular lines on the top or the sides of frosted cakes, always applying even pressure as you draw the comb over the surface. Treat the combs with care. They must be perfectly flat with straight teeth to do a good job.

DECORATING WITH PIPED FROSTING

PIPING TOOLS

Pastry tips, or tubes, used with pastry bags (also known as piping or icing bags) come in a wealth of shapes and sizes, as do the bags. Many tips are for piping specific decorations such as rose petals or ruffles. But just a handful of plain and star tips provides a wide variety of decorating possibilities. You can decorate any cake in this collection with only five tips: ⅜ inch (9 mm), ½ inch (12 mm), and ¾ inch (2 cm) star, plus ⅜ inch (9 mm) and ½ inch (12 mm) plain. Look for pastry tips in cookware and baking-supply stores or through mail-order sources.

Set aside about 1 cup (8 fl oz/225 ml) of the frosting before frosting the entire cake. To fill a pastry bag, fit a tip into the bottom of the bag. Twist the bag just above the tip and push the bag into the tip, to prevent the frosting from dripping out. Hold the bag in one hand and fold down the top third of the bag over your curved fingers, making a cuff. Using a large rubber spatula, carefully put the frosting into the bag without getting any on the outside of the bag. Unfold the cuff and pleat the top closed to meet the frosting. Pull the tip to free the twisted bag and, while holding the pleated top, use a twisting motion to push the frosting into the tip of the bag. Squeeze the top of the bag with one hand and guide the tip with the other hand.

To make rosettes, spirals, and shells, use a star tip of any size *(left).* For rosettes, hold the pastry bag perpendicular to and about 1 inch (2.5 cm) from the cake. Squeeze a small amount of frosting onto the cake to the desired size, then stop pressing and pull the bag up to make a point (see Raspberry Charlotte, page 67). For spirals, hold the pastry bag at a 45-degree angle and about 1 inch (2.5 cm) from the cake. Squeeze frosting onto the cake, moving the bag in a spiral (see Chocolate-Orange Cupcakes, page 32). For shells, hold the pastry bag perpendicular to the top edge of the cake and with the tip just touching the cake. As you squeeze the bag, lift the tip and then return it alongside the starting point, to form a loop of frosting. Make connecting loops around the cake (see Lemon Sponge Cake, page 60).

To make a plain beaded border on a cake *(opposite),* use a plain tip of any size. Hold the pastry bag about 1 inch (2.5) from the cake and perpendicular to the top edge. Squeeze a bead, then stop. Squeeze another bead next to the previous one. Continue until the top edge is ringed with beads.

MAKES 1 DECORATED CAKE

1 frosted cake (page 60)

Buttercream, whipped cream, or other frosting for decorating

PIPING WITH CHOCOLATE

1 frosted cake (page 18)

2 oz (60 g) semisweet (plain) or bittersweet chocolate, finely chopped

Put the chopped chocolate in a clean, dry stainless-steel bowl. Set the bowl in a saucepan over, but not touching, barely simmering water. Heat the chocolate, stirring occasionally, until it melts and is free of lumps (page 32).

Using parchment (baking) paper, cut a triangle with two sides about 7½ inches (19 cm) and one about 10½ inches (26.5 cm) and make a cone *(right)* for piping the chocolate. Using a teaspoon, fill the cone half full with the melted chocolate. Fold down the top to close the cone. With sharp scissors, cut a small hole in the tip of the filled cone. When piping, squeeze the cone with one hand and steady that hand with the other. Move your entire arm, not just your fingers.

To make a lace pattern, pipe a line around the area to be filled with the pattern. Pipe squiggly lines in a random pattern to fill in the space (see Hazelnut Cake with Chocolate Glaze, page 54).

To make a spiderweb, pipe concentric circles, 1 inch (2.5 cm) apart, on top of the cake. Lightly drag a toothpick or the tip of a paring knife through all the circles, from the center of the cake to the outside edge at 1-inch (2.5-cm) intervals, wiping the toothpick or knife with a damp paper towel after each stroke.

To make a crosshatch pattern, pipe parallel lines ½ inch (12 mm) apart on the top of the cake. Rotate the cake 90 degrees and pipe another set of parallel lines *(opposite)*.

MAKES 1 DECORATED CAKE

MAKING A PAPER CONE

Using your left thumb and fore-finger, hold the middle of the long side of the triangle so it is toward you. With your right hand, grasp the right tip of the triangle and curl it upward to meet the tip pointing away from you. You will have created a conical shape using half of the triangle. Hold the two tips with your right thumb and forefinger. Grasping the remaining tip with your left thumb and forefinger, wrap the remaining half of the triangle around the conical shape to make a cone with a sharp point, adjusting the paper as necessary. Fold the tips inside. Secure the cone with a piece of tape.

MAKING CHOCOLATE DECORATIONS

To make chocolate curls, wrap the chocolate bar in plastic wrap. Rub between your hands for 1–2 minutes or microwave it on low for 5 seconds. Remove the plastic and, using a vegetable peeler, scrape the blade lengthwise across the bar to create delicate curls of chocolate, allowing them to fall on a sheet of waxed paper. If the curls come off in flakes, the chocolate is too cold; warm it again before continuing. If you are not using the curls right away, set them aside at room temperature. For longer storage, place them in an airtight container in the refrigerator for up to 2 weeks. To decorate a cake, place the curls with a small offset frosting spatula rather than your hands, which might melt the chocolate (see Black Forest Cake, page 22).

To make chocolate petals, tape a sheet of plastic wrap onto a baking sheet. Put the chopped chocolate in a clean, dry stainless-steel bowl. Set the bowl in a saucepan over, but not touching, barely simmering water (page 32). Gently heat the chocolate, stirring occasionally, until it melts and registers 90°F (32°C) on an instant-read thermometer. (Failing to heat the chocolate to the correct temperature may cause it to streak.) Remove from the heat. For large petals, dip the tip of a frosting spatula 1½ inches (4 cm) wide into the chocolate, then spread a thin band about 1 inch (2.5 cm) long on the plastic wrap. Continue making the petals, dipping the spatula in the chocolate for each one. Refrigerate the petals until firm, about 10 minutes. For small petals, use a spatula ¾ inch (2 cm) wide. Store in an airtight plastic container in the refrigerator for up to 2 weeks.

To decorate a cake, using a small offset frosting spatula, carefully remove the petals from the plastic wrap. Arrange them on the cake, touching them as little as possible.

MAKES ABOUT 1 CUP (8 OZ/225 G) CURLS OR ABOUT 80 PETALS

FOR CHOCOLATE CURLS:

1 bar (about 8 oz/225 g) semisweet (plain) or bittersweet chocolate

FOR CHOCOLATE PETALS:

3 oz (85 g) bittersweet chocolate, finely chopped

CHOCOLATE PETALS

Once you have mastered the technique of forming chocolate petals, you can use them to create various shapes on cakes. Small or large petals may be set in a circle around the top edge of a round cake or in a line down the center of a long cake. You can also form a flower by arranging the petals in a circle. The petals should be set side by side, slightly overlapping and at the same angle, on top of a cake *(opposite)*. If desired, add a center to each flower by piping a rosette of buttercream or other frosting in the middle (page 98).

CANDYING FRESH FLOWERS AND CITRUS ZEST

FOR CANDIED FLOWERS:

**1 large egg white,
at room temperature**

**20–50 pesticide-free
fresh flowers** *(far right)*

Granulated sugar

FOR CANDIED ZEST:

2 oranges

1 lemon

**1½ cups (10½ oz/300 g)
plus ⅓ cup (2½ oz/70 g)
granulated sugar**

**¾ cup (6 fl oz/170 ml)
water**

**1 tablespoon fresh
lemon juice**

To make candied flowers, line a baking sheet with parchment (baking) paper. In a bowl, beat the egg white until it is covered with a light foam. Using a clean, small paintbrush, lightly and evenly coat the flowers with egg white. Sprinkle them with sugar. If the sugar is absorbed after a few minutes, sprinkle again. Put the flowers on the paper and let dry at room temperature for 24 hours. Use your fingers to transfer them carefully to a cake. They will keep for up to 3 days stored between layers of waxed paper in an airtight container at room temperature.

To make candied zest, thoroughly wash the oranges and lemon. Cut a slice from the blossom end of each fruit so it stands upright on a work surface. Working from top to bottom, use a small, sharp knife to cut strips of zest, leaving the white pith behind. Stack the strips and cut them lengthwise into narrow strips ¼ inch (6 mm) wide. Bring a saucepan of water to boil. Add the zest strips and cook for 5 minutes. Drain the zest, refill the pan with water, and repeat. In another saucepan over medium heat, bring the 1½ cups sugar, ¾ cup water, and lemon juice to a boil, stirring occasionally. Add the zest strips, reduce the heat to very low (barely a simmer), and cook until the strips are translucent and tender, about 30 minutes. With a fork, lift the strips from the syrup and place on a wire rack set over waxed paper, making sure that the strips are not touching. Let dry overnight at room temperature.

Put the ⅓ cup sugar in a small, wide bowl. Toss the zest, about 10 strips at a time, in the sugar. If not using the zest immediately, store in an airtight container. It will keep for up to 1 month at room temperature.

Note: Candying flowers calls for uncooked egg whites. For more information, see page 109.

MAKES 20–30 CANDIED FLOWERS OR ABOUT ½ CUP (3 OZ/85 G) CANDIED ZEST

EDIBLE FLOWERS

Various edible fresh flowers may be candied for decorating or garnishing cakes. The best choices are small blossoms with simple configurations of petals that can easily be brushed with egg white and coated with granules of sugar. These include violets, pansies, small roses, and Peruvian lilies. It is especially important to look for flowers grown without pesticides. Farmers' markets are one source for untreated flowers. You can also grow your own or obtain them from a friend's home garden. If you cannot verify that a flower is edible or is pesticide free, it is best not to use it.

CAKE BASICS

Some cakes depend on just a handful of basic ingredients and a few easy techniques. Others are labor-intensive creations with multiple layers, elegant fillings, and billowy frostings. No matter which recipe you choose, here are some tips to help you make it perfectly.

MISE EN PLACE

The French phrase *mise en place,* literally "putting in place," is a governing rule of cake making that calls for measuring all the ingredients before beginning a recipe. But the *mise en place* should start even before you do your measuring. First, read the recipe from start to finish to make sure that you have all the ingredients on hand, that you understand the order in which you will be using them, and that you have a sense of the flow of the steps. At the same time, check to see that you have all the necessary tools and the correct size of pan or pans (page 112). Next, read up on any techniques, such as folding, whipping egg whites, or using a pastry bag, that are new to you or for which you need a little refresher course. Then, when you are sure that making the cake will have your undivided attention, you are ready to proceed.

INGREDIENTS

Most recipes call for a relatively small number of everyday ingredients. The taste of a finished cake reflects what went into it, so always use the freshest, highest-quality ingredients available.

FLOUR

Two general types of wheat are grown: hard wheat, which is high in protein, and soft wheat, which has less protein and more starch. Protein allows a dough to form an extendable network of interlacing strands, or gluten. It is what gives a dough elasticity when it is kneaded, a characteristic that is good for bread, but bad for cakes, making them tough. In contrast to bread doughs, cake batters are usually manipulated as little as possible once the flour is added.

Cakes are made with all-purpose (plain) flour or cake (soft-wheat) flour. All-purpose flour, a blend of hard- and soft-wheat flours, is suited for a wide range of baked goods, including many cakes. Cake flour, milled finer and with less gluten, is better for delicate cakes, as it results in a finer crumb.

Freshly milled flour has an ivory cast. Cake flour is bleached to make it whiter for aesthetic reasons. This process also reduces the amount of protein slightly. All-purpose flour is available both bleached and unbleached. Some bakers prefer to use only unbleached flour to avoid an unnecessary chemical and because they believe they can taste the difference in the finished cake.

SUGAR

Processed from either sugarcane or sugar beets, sugar comes in several forms used by bakers. Granulated sugar is more than 99 percent pure sucrose, a double sugar composed of glucose and fructose. It not only adds sweetness to cakes, but also keeps them moist and helps them brown. Granulated sugar contributes to a cake's final texture as well, especially butter cakes. When butter and sugar are beaten together, the first step in making a butter cake, the sharp crystals help trap air, which adds to the cake's final volume. Sugar also helps stabilize whipped egg whites.

A syrup forms when sugar and water are heated together. If a flavoring, such as a liqueur or a citrus extract (essence), is added to the syrup, it can be brushed onto a cake for moisture and flavor. If the sugar and water are boiled, the syrup loses moisture, becoming more concentrated. Once the syrup reaches 250°F (120°C) on a candy thermometer, it can be slowly poured into egg whites during whipping, to make a glossy, firm meringue. If you continue to cook the syrup beyond 250°F, it will eventually turn a deep caramel color, and can be made into a sauce with the addition of a hot liquid.

Superfine sugar, also known as caster sugar, is granulated sugar ground to finer crystals. Because the crystals are smaller, they dissolve more quickly, making superfine sugar ideal for use in delicate cake batters and for beating egg whites.

Confectioners' sugar, also known as powdered sugar or icing sugar, is granulated sugar that has been crushed to a powder. Some manufacturers mix a small amount of cornstarch (cornflour) into the sugar to prevent clumping. Because it dissolves quickly, confectioners' sugar is often folded into beaten egg whites in the final stage of making a meringue or beaten into whipped cream. A delicate sifting of confectioners' sugar over meringues or ladyfingers (page 113) just before they go into the oven helps them hold their shape during baking. A similar dusting is sometimes used to decorate finished cakes (page 94).

Brown sugar contains dark cane syrup, which gives it color and flavor. The sugar has a moist texture and rich taste that complement gingerbread (page 79) and spice cakes (page 40). Brown sugar comes in two types, golden and dark; their differences depend on the amount and type of syrup used in their production.

Molasses is a sweet, dark liquid made from either cane juice or syrup obtained from washing cane sugar crystals at a refinery. It is heated to crystallize the sugar, which is then removed. The resulting liquid is pasteurized and filtered to produce light molasses. The liquid can be heated and crystallized more than once; the molasses becomes darker and less sweet each time. Manufacturers blend these liquids to make dark or blackstrap molasses. The darker the molasses, the more robust the taste.

BUTTER

Most of the butter available is lightly salted to extend its shelf life. For baking, however, always use unsalted butter. It has a fresher, creamier taste, and it allows you to control the amount of salt in your cake batters.

Many creameries are making butter with an elevated fat content, sometimes as high as 86 percent. Often labeled "European style," this butter contains less water, and cakes made with it tend to have a richer, moister, more velvety texture. More important than a butter's fat content is its taste, so always choose the butter that tastes the best to you.

Most cakes call for butter at room temperature. Cold butter is more difficult to beat, and it can cause a batter to separate when eggs are added to it.

EGGS

Eggs play multiple—and critical—roles in cake baking. The yolks encourage batters to emulsify and contribute to a tender crumb, and the whites give cakes much of their structure. The tiny bubbles trapped in whipped whites help cakes to rise. Always bring egg whites for whipping to room temperature to ensure that they reach their optimal height. If you have forgotten to remove them from the refrigerator in time, warm them in their shells in a bowl of hot tap water before you separate them. Never overbeat whites, and never overfold beaten whites into batters. Both actions will deflate the bubbles that guarantee loft.

The whole eggs that go into a cake batter should be at room temperature as well. Cold eggs can cause butter to congeal, and the batter to separate.

Eggs are sized according to weight. For example, a dozen large eggs in the shell weigh 24 ounces (670 g), while an equal number of extra-large eggs weighs 27 ounces (755 g). All the recipes in this book call for large eggs. Do not substitute another size, or the outcome may be disappointing. Refrigerate eggs as soon as you get them home, and use them by their sell-by date, which is 30 days beyond their packing date.

Today, many cooks are concerned about the possible presence of the bacteria salmonella in eggs. Cooking eggs at 140°F (60°C) for 3 minutes, or to an end temperature of 160°F (71°C), will kill any salmonella present. Small children, the elderly, pregnant women, and people with compromised immune systems should not eat undercooked or raw eggs. Raw egg whites are used only once in this book, in the candied flower recipe (page 105). For those concerned about egg safety, use pasteurized whites in place of raw in this recipe.

VANILLA EXTRACT

Pure vanilla extract (essence) is obtained from a tropical vine, a member of a large orchid family, in a laborious process. Pods resembling green beans are harvested when they are nine months old and then cured to develop their distinctive taste. Finally, their flavor is extracted by steeping them in alcohol. Many types of vanilla exist, but the two most important for bakers are Bourbon-Madagascar and Tahitian. Both are aromatic and flavorful, with the Tahitian having more floral tones. Vanillin, imitation vanilla, is a poor substitute for the real thing.

TECHNIQUES

A few basic techniques are used in the making of nearly every cake, and every baker must master them in order to make beautiful and delicious cakes.

WEIGHING AND MEASURING

Successful baking depends on accuracy, so having the correct amount of each ingredient is crucial. Weighing dry ingredients is more accurate than measuring in cups, and a scale is a good investment if you bake often. If you use cup measures, however, keep these points in mind: Measuring cups for dry measure and liquid measure are not interchangeable. Dry measuring cups are metal or heavy-duty plastic and have straight sides, while liquid measuring cups are clear glass or plastic, look like pitchers, and have vertical markings indicating amounts on their sides.

When measuring a dry ingredient, such as flour or sugar, spoon up the ingredient and place it in a measuring cup without tamping it down, then level the top with the blunt edge of a knife. Measuring spoons can be dipped into the container, then leveled. Brown sugar should be tightly packed into the measuring cup. To measure liquid, pour the liquid into the cup, then read it at eye level.

Dry ingredients are sometimes sifted to aerate them or to combine them. A sifter or a fine-mesh sieve will do the job. Sifting onto waxed paper eliminates cleaning a bowl.

BAKING CAKES

A few tips will ensure a perfectly baked cake every time: First, the temperature inside an oven often does not agree with the thermostat setting. Put an oven thermometer on the rack where the cake is baking to determine your oven's accuracy, then adjust the thermostat accordingly. Also, no oven bakes evenly, so learn your oven's hot spots. Always rotate pans 180 degrees halfway through baking, whether or not a recipe instructs you to do so, to ensure a more even bake, especially when using large rectangular pans. The heat is more even in the middle of an oven, so bake cakes on the middle rack. Unless stated otherwise in the recipe, cool cakes in their pans on a wire rack for about 10 minutes before unmolding them.

FROSTING A LAYER CAKE

To protect the plate, place 4 waxed paper strips under and along the edges of the bottom layer. Then arrange the layers and filling as directed in the recipe. Use a straight frosting spatula as long as the diameter of the cake. Dip it in warm water after each stroke and wipe it dry (a warm spatula will smooth the frosting easier than a cold one). Follow the steps shown opposite for frosting the cake:

1 **Applying a crumb coat**: Using a dry pastry brush, gently whisk away loose crumbs from the top and sides. Put no more than a third of the frosting on top of the cake. Smooth it over the top and down the sides to cover the entire surface. This thin coating will adhere the crumbs to the surface.

2 **Frosting the top**: If some of the frosting will be used to decorate the finished cake, set aside the amount indicated in the recipe. Put the remaining frosting in the center of the top of the cake and smooth it evenly. The frosting will cover the top in a thick layer.

3 **Covering the sides**: Evenly smooth the frosting from the top of the cake down the sides, turning the cake as you work. As you cover the sides, hold the spatula almost perpendicular to the top of the cake.

4 **Smoothing the frosting**: Holding the spatula almost horizontal to the cake's top, smooth the top with long strokes. Then run the spatula around the sides, making the frosting as smooth as possible. Using short strokes, remove excess frosting from the edge of the top. Discard the waxed paper strips.

A decorating turntable makes frosting a cake easier. The turntable is made up of a metal or plastic plate, round or rectangular, that sits on a base with a rotating mechanism, much like a lazy Susan. Put the filled cake on its plate on the turntable and proceed as described above, rotating the turntable with one hand as you hold the spatula in the other.

SERVING CAKES

Serve cakes at room temperature to appreciate their flavor fully. Exceptions are cakes with gelatin, such as mousse cakes, which should be refrigerated until serving so that they remain firm, and cakes frosted with whipped cream.

Use a sharp, serrated knife or a sharp, thin-bladed knife to cut cakes. Delicate, airy cakes, such as chiffon and angel food, are difficult to cut because they are so pliable; a serrated knife and a gentle sawing motion work best.

If a cake is frosted or filled, or if it is a cheesecake, dip the knife blade in water and wipe it clean after each cut.

EQUIPMENT

In addition to such basics as a flour sifter, mixing bowls, measuring cups and spoons, and various cake pans as described below, you will want to have other equipment on hand for making cakes. The recipes in this book are prepared with a stand mixer. The mixer has a deep mixing bowl and comes with three attachments: a paddle, for creaming butter and combining wet and dry ingredients, among other functions; a whisk, for whipping egg whites or heavy (double) cream; and a dough hook, for kneading yeast-leavened dough like the one in Babas au Rhum (page 83). You can also use a metal balloon whisk to incorporate air into whipped cream or egg whites.

A large rubber spatula is essential for combining mixtures of disparate densities, such as whipped cream and a fruit purée or other flavoring, and for folding amendments such as nuts into a batter. Straight frosting spatulas and offset frosting spatulas are also useful. The former are flexible, flat metal spatulas; choose one with a blade as long as the diameter of the cake you will be frosting. The metal blades of offset spatulas are set at an angle from the handles. This design is useful not only for frosting cakes but also for smoothing batters after they are poured into cake pans. Both types are also called icing spatulas.

Finally, if you are making decorated cakes, you will want to acquire a decorating comb (page 97) and piping tools, including a pastry bag and a basic selection of tips (page 98).

CAKE PANS

The shape of a cake adds to its visual appeal. Although many cakes in this book are baked in 9-inch (23-cm) round pans, either 2 or 3 inches (5 or 7.5 cm) deep, others take different forms. Both the Carrot Cake (page 17) and the Caramelized Pear Upside-Down Gingerbread (page 79) are baked in square pans. Square serving pieces seem more traditional for a flat carrot cake, and a square gingerbread is easier to cut.

Rectangular pans, such as baking sheets, give bakers choices for assembling cakes. You can cut the cake into smaller rectangles, then layer the rectangles with a filling to make a low, elegant cake, such as the Hazelnut Cake with Chocolate Glaze (page 54). You can use the same pan to bake a thin sheet, which is the base for the two rolled cakes in this book (pages 52 and 71). Rectangular pans are also used to bake the meringues for the Hazelnut Dacquoises (page 47) and Chocolate Vacherins (page 51).

A springform pan, a round pan outfitted with a clamp that releases the sides from the base, is useful for baking particularly solid cakes, such as cheesecakes, that otherwise would be difficult to unmold. It can also be used for assembling mousse cakes (page 84). Tall tube pans are ideal vessels for the light, delicate batters of chiffon and angel food cakes, both of which depend on the center tube for even baking and for support as they rise. Loaf pans are perfect for pound cakes (page 31) and other loaf cakes such as Date-Walnut Loaf (page 76). Standard muffin pans, with cups 2½ inches (6 cm) wide and 1¼ inches (3 cm) deep, are just the right size for cupcakes (page 32). Bundt pans, deep tube pans with sculptured sides, transfer their decorative shapes to the cakes baked in them.

Several special pans are called for in this book: A savarin mold, a low ring mold traditionally used for baking a yeast-risen, syrup-soaked cake of the same name, takes another role here and bakes the Chocolate-Almond Cake with Caramel Sauce (page 44). Baba molds, individual cups with sloping sides, are used for making syrup-soaked Babas au Rhum (page 83). Popover molds, which are similar in size and shape and rest in a rack for carrying, are more readily available and can take their place. A brioche mold, with its deeply fluted sides, is used to bake the Cinnamon-Applesauce Cake (page 28) and to assemble the Eggnog Bavarian Cream Cake (page 87). A deep, round charlotte mold, with its modestly flared sides, houses the Raspberry Charlotte (page 67) and is also used to bake the cake that becomes the Cloche Café (page 48).

Simple metal pans come in all these shapes. Dark metal pans absorb heat more readily than light metal ones, and thus tend to bake faster. Glass or ceramic pans also conduct and retain heat well, which can result in overbrowning. Finally, many pans are coated with a nonstick lining, which makes cakes easier to unmold, but can heighten browning as well. In all cases, keep an eye on your cakes, as you may need to reduce baking temperatures and times slightly.

PREPARING PANS

With the exception of tube pans used to bake chiffon or angel food cakes, which need fat-free surfaces to help them rise, cake pans are lined with parchment (baking) paper or buttered to aid unmolding. If the pan has straight sides, such as a 9-inch (23-cm) round cake pan, line the bottom with a disk of parchment paper cut to fit precisely, then run a table knife around the sides of the cooled cake just before unmolding it. Lining rectangular pans with parchment paper also eases unmolding these large cakes. Generously coat pans with sculptured sides, such as Bundt pans, with soft, not melted, butter.

BASIC RECIPES

LADYFINGERS

5 large eggs, separated, plus 1 large egg yolk, at room temperature

⅔ cup (4½ oz/125 g) granulated sugar

1 cup (4½ oz/125 g) unbleached all-purpose (plain) flour, sifted

Confectioners' (icing) sugar for dusting

Preheat the oven to 400°F (200°C). If making the ladyfingers for Raspberry Charlotte (page 67), draw 2 pairs of lines, spacing each pair 3 inches (7.5 cm) apart (almost the height of an 8-cup/64–fl oz/1.8-l charlotte mold), down the length of a piece of parchment (baking) paper large enough to fit on a 12-by-18-by-1-inch (30-by-45-by-2.5-cm) baking sheet. You should have 4 lines. On another piece of parchment paper, use the bottom and top of the mold to trace 2 circles. One circle will be smaller than the other. Put the papers, marked sides down, on baking sheets.

Using a stand mixer, beat the egg whites with the whisk on medium speed until they start to foam. Add a third of the granulated sugar and beat until the whites are opaque, then add another third of the sugar. When the whites start to increase in volume and become firm, add the remaining sugar and increase the speed to high. Beat until the whites form soft peaks but still look wet. In a bowl, whisk the yolks by hand until blended. Using a large rubber spatula, carefully fold the yolks into the beaten whites. Sift half of the flour over the egg mixture and carefully fold in. Repeat with the remaining flour.

Fill a pastry bag fitted with a ¾-inch (2-cm) plain tip with the batter (page 98). Pipe concentric circles to fill the 2 circles on the parchment paper. Pipe 3-inch (7.5-cm) strips of batter, with the edges just barely touching, between each set of lines on the other piece of paper. You should have about 24 ladyfingers. The ladyfingers will spread as they bake and adhere together, but still retain their individual shapes. Using a fine-mesh sieve, dust the circles and strips with a fine layer of confectioners' sugar. Bake until the batter is puffed, lightly browned, and slightly cracked, 10–12 minutes. Transfer the sheet to a wire rack and let the ladyfingers cool completely. Makes about 24 ladyfingers, plus 2 cake rounds.

Variation Tip: To make chocolate ladyfingers for the Eggnog Bavarian Cream Cake (page 87), follow the instructions above using 3 large eggs, separated; ½ cup (3½ oz/100 g) granulated sugar; and ½ cup (2½ oz/70 g) unbleached all-purpose (plain) flour. Sift 2 tablespoons Dutch-process cocoa powder (page 13) together with the flour. You will need one baking sheet and one length of parchment paper marked as described above with 2 sets of lines, each set spaced 3 inches (7.5 cm) apart. Makes about 20 chocolate ladyfingers.

PASTRY CREAM

1 cup (8 fl oz/225 ml) milk

5 tablespoons (2½ oz/70 g) sugar

3 large egg yolks

2 tablespoons cornstarch (cornflour)

1 teaspoon vanilla extract (essence)

In a small saucepan over medium heat, heat ¾ cup (6 fl oz/170 ml) of the milk and 2 tablespoons of the sugar, stirring to dissolve the sugar, until small bubbles appear along the edge of the pan. Meanwhile, in a bowl, whisk together the egg yolks and the remaining 3 tablespoons sugar until well combined. In a small bowl, whisk together the remaining ¼ cup (2 fl oz/55 ml) milk and the cornstarch, then whisk into the yolk mixture.

Pour the hot milk mixture into the yolk mixture in a slow, steady stream, whisking constantly, then return the mixture to the pan. Bring to a boil over medium heat, whisking constantly. Whisk in the vanilla. Pour the pastry cream into a bowl, cover with plastic wrap, and refrigerate until needed, or for up to 4 days. Makes about 1 cup (8 fl oz/225 ml).

CARAMEL SAUCE

¾ cup (6 fl oz/170 ml) water

1 cup (7 oz/200 g) sugar

1 cup (8 fl oz/225 ml) heavy (double) cream

In a large, heavy saucepan over medium heat, bring ¼ cup (2 fl oz/60 ml) of the water and the sugar to a boil, stirring a few times until the sugar dissolves. Using a damp pastry brush, brush down any crystals that form on the sides of the pan. Cook the syrup, undisturbed, over medium-high heat until it is a light caramel color, 5–10 minutes. Turn off the heat.

Meanwhile, in a saucepan over medium heat, bring the remaining ½ cup (4 fl oz/110 ml) water to a boil. In another saucepan over medium heat, heat the cream just until it comes to a boil, then immediately remove from the heat. Wearing oven mitts, carefully whisk the cream into the syrup in 3 additions; it will bubble up dramatically. Whisk in the boiling water in 3 additions. Let the sauce cool, then cover and refrigerate until needed, or for up to 1 week. Makes 1 cup (8 fl oz/225 ml).

COFFEE MERINGUE BUTTERCREAM

¾ cup (6 oz/170 g) unsalted butter, at room temperature

3 large egg whites, at room temperature

¾ cup (5½ oz/155 g) plus 3 tablespoons sugar

3 tablespoons water

4 teaspoons instant espresso powder, dissolved in 1 teaspoon boiling water

In a bowl, whisk the butter by hand until it is creamy.

Using a stand mixer, beat the egg whites with the whisk on medium speed until they start to foam. Add 2 tablespoons of the sugar and beat until the whites become opaque and then increase in volume.

Meanwhile, make a sugar syrup: In a saucepan over medium heat, bring the ¾ cup sugar and 3 tablespoons water to a boil, stirring a few times until the sugar dissolves. Using a damp pastry brush, brush down any crystals that form on the sides of the pan. Cook the syrup, undisturbed, over medium-high heat until it registers 240°F (115°C) on a candy thermometer. While continuing to boil the syrup, increase the mixer speed to high and add the remaining 1 tablespoon sugar to the egg whites.

When the syrup registers 250°F (120°C), remove it from the heat. With the mixer speed on high, pour the syrup into the whites in a thin stream, aiming for the side of the bowl. Reduce the speed to medium and beat until the meringue cools to room temperature and is stiff, about 5 minutes.

Beat in the dissolved espresso, then beat in the butter in 3 additions, incorporating each addition before adding another. When all the butter has been added, reduce the speed to medium-high and beat the buttercream until thick and smooth, about 1 minute.

The buttercream should be used immediately. Makes 2½ cups (20 fl oz/560 ml).

Variation Tip: To make buttercream for the Devil's Food Cake (page 13), use 1 cup (8 oz/ 225 g) unsalted butter; 5 large egg whites; and 5 tablespoons (2½ oz/70 g) sugar; and 2 tablespoons plus ½ teaspoon instant espresso powder dissolved in 2 teaspoons boiling water. For the sugar syrup, use 1¼ cups (9 oz/250 g) sugar and 5 tablespoons (2½ fl oz/70 ml) water. Add 3 tablespoons of the sugar to the egg whites after they foam and the remaining 2 tablespoons after increasing the mixer speed to high. Makes about 4 cups (32 fl oz/900 ml).

VANILLA BUTTERCREAM

1½ cups (12 oz/335 g) unsalted butter, at room temperature

½ cup (4 fl oz/110 ml) whole milk

¾ cup (6 oz/160 g) sugar

5 large egg yolks

2 teaspoons vanilla extract (essence)

Using a stand mixer, beat the butter with the paddle on medium speed until it is the consistency of mayonnaise. It should not be melted. Transfer to another bowl and thoroughly wash and dry the mixer bowl. In a saucepan over medium heat, heat the milk and ¼ cup (2 oz/60 g) of the sugar, stirring occasionally, until small bubbles appear along the edge of the pan.

Meanwhile, using the stand mixer, beat the egg yolks and the remaining ½ cup (4 oz/100 g) sugar with the whisk on medium-high speed until the mixture is pale and thick, about 3 minutes. Reduce the speed to low and pour in the hot milk mixture in a thin stream. Return the mixture to the saucepan. Thoroughly wash and dry the mixer bowl and whisk.

Cook over medium heat, whisking constantly, until it registers 170°F (77°C) on an instant-read thermometer, 5–7 minutes. Pour the mixture back into the mixer bowl and beat with the whisk on medium speed until cool, 5–10 minutes. Beat in the vanilla. Add the butter in 4 additions, incorporating each addition before adding another. Use immediately, or refrigerate until needed, or for up to 3 days. If the buttercream has been refrigerated, whisk it by hand over simmering water until it reaches spreading consistency. Makes 3 cups (24 fl oz/670 ml), enough for a 2-layer 9-inch (23-cm) cake.

Variation Tips: To make Lemon Buttercream, substitute 1 tablespoon lemon extract (essence) for the vanilla. To make Chocolate Buttercream, melt 4 oz (110 g) bittersweet chocolate, finely chopped, over simmering water (page 32). Let cool to room temperature. Omit the vanilla and beat the melted chocolate into the buttercream instead.

RASPBERRY PURÉE

4 cups (12 oz/335 g) raspberries

3 tablespoons confectioners' (icing) sugar

In a food processor or blender, purée the raspberries with the sugar. Strain through a fine-mesh sieve into a bowl, pressing on the mixture with the back of a spoon. Refrigerate until needed, or for up to 3 days. Remove from the refrigerator 30 minutes before serving. Makes 1 cup (8 fl oz/225 ml).

LEMON CURD

Grated zest of 1 lemon (page 88)

6 tablespoons (3 fl oz/85 ml) fresh lemon juice

3 tablespoons fresh orange juice

2 large eggs

⅓ cup (2½ oz/70 g) sugar

2 tablespoons unsalted butter

2 tablespoons heavy (double) cream

In a saucepan over medium heat, combine the lemon zest, lemon and orange juices, eggs, sugar, butter, and cream. Cook, whisking constantly, until the curd thickens and registers 165°F (74°C) on an instant-read thermometer, about 5 minutes. Watch the curd carefully and do not overcook it. Immediately pour the curd into a bowl, cover with plastic wrap, and refrigerate until needed, or for up to 1 week. Makes 1 cup (8 fl oz/225 ml).

INDEX

SIMON & SCHUSTER SOURCE
A Division of Simon & Schuster, Inc.
Rockefeller Center
1230 Avenue of the Americas
New York, NY 10020

WILLIAMS-SONOMA
Founder and Vice-Chairman: Chuck Williams

WELDON OWEN INC.
Chief Executive Officer: John Owen
President: Terry Newell
Chief Operating Officer: Larry Partington
Vice President, International Sales: Stuart Laurence
Creative Director: Gaye Allen
Associate Creative Director: Leslie Harrington
Series Editor: Sarah Putman Clegg
Managing Editor: Judith Dunham
Editor: Heather Belt
Designer: Teri Gardiner
Production Director: Chris Hemesath
Color Manager: Teri Bell
Shipping and Production Coordinator: Libby Temple

Weldon Owen wishes to thank the following
people for their generous assistance and support
in producing this book: Copy Editor Kris Balloun;
Consulting Editor Sharon Silva; Food Stylist Sandra
Cook; Assistant Food Stylists Elisabet der
Nederlanden, Melinda Barsales, and Annie Salisbury;
Recipe Consultant Peggy Fallon; Photographer's
Assistants Noriko Akiyama and Heidi Ladendorf;
Proofreaders Desne Ahlers and Carrie Bradley;
Production Designer Linda Bouchard;
and Indexer Ken DellaPenta.

Williams-Sonoma Collection *Cake* was
conceived and produced by Weldon Owen Inc.,
814 Montgomery Street, San Francisco,
California 94133, in collaboration with
Williams-Sonoma, 3250 Van Ness Avenue,
San Francisco, California 94109

A Weldon Owen Production

For information regarding special discounts for
bulk purchases, please contact Simon & Schuster
Special Sales at 1-800-456-6798 or
business@simonandschuster.com

Set in Trajan, Utopia, and Vectora.

Color separations by Bright Arts Graphics
Singapore (Pte.) Ltd.
Printed and bound in Singapore by Tien Wah
Press (Pte.) Ltd.

First printed in 2003.

10 9 8 7 6 5

Library of Congress Cataloging-in-Publication Data

Gage, Fran.
   Cake / recipes and text, Fran Gage ; general
editor, Chuck Williams ; photographs, Noel
Barnhurst.
       p. cm. — (Williams-Sonoma collection)
   At head of title: Williams-Sonoma.
   Includes index.
   1. Cake I. Title: Williams-Sonoma cake.
II. Williams, Chuck. III. Title. IV. Williams-Sonoma
collection (New York, N.Y.)
TX771.G34 2003
641.8'653—dc21
                                      2003048344
ISBN 0-7432-5020-6

A NOTE ON WEIGHTS AND MEASURES

All recipes include customary U.S. and metric measurements. Metric conversions are based on
a standard developed for this book and have been rounded off. Actual weights may vary.